When Homosexuality Hits Home

Joe Dallas

HARVEST HOUSE PUBLISHERS
EUGENE, OREGON

Unless otherwise indicated, all Scripture quotations are from the New King James Version. Copyright ©1982 by Thomas Nelson, Inc. Used by permission. All rights reserved.

Verses marked KJV are from the King James Version of the Bible.

Cover by Knail, Salem, Oregon

Cover photo © Thinkstock / Zoonar / Photographer: Markus Gann, Fotolia / schantalao

WHEN HOMOSEXUALITY HITS HOME
Copyright © 2004, 2015 by Joe Dallas
Published by Harvest House Publishers
Eugene, Oregon 97402
www.harvesthousepublishers.com

ISBN 978-0-7369-6205-6 (pbk.)
ISBN 978-0-7369-6206-3 (eBook)

Library of Congress Cataloging-in-Publication Data
Dallas, Joe, 1954-
When homosexuality hits home / Joe Dallas.
    p. cm.
ISBN 0-7369-1201-0 (pbk.)
1. Homosexuality—Religious aspects—Christianity. I. Title.
BR115.H6D37 2004
261.8'35766—dc22   2004007303

Printed in the United States of America

19 20 21 22 23 / VP-KB / 10 9 8 7 6 5 4

To my family,
and to all our families.

Acknowledgments

My thanks to Nick Harrison of Harvest House Publishers for his patience and persistence when editing this project.

As always, my gratitude to Renee, Jody, and Jeremy for their unending love and support is greater than I can express.

Contents

*Each of us will at some point in our lives look upon
a loved one and ask the question:*

"We are willing, Lord, but what can we do?"

*For it is true that we can seldom help those closest to us. Either
we don't know what part of ourselves to give, or, more often
than not, the part we have to give is not wanted.
And so it is those we live with, and should know, who elude us.
But we can still love them. We can love completely,
without complete understanding.*

—A RIVER RUNS THROUGH IT

Introduction

'll begin by assuming you never thought you'd be reading a book like this.

That's a broad assumption, of course, and I make it without knowing you or the circumstances that put this book in your hands. Still, I can safely guess that someone you love is homosexual. Further, you probably know this book is written from a conservative Christian viewpoint, so if you've picked it up, I'll wager you do not approve of homosexuality, but care deeply about your gay loved one nonetheless. I also assume you'd like to protect your relationship with him or her without compromising your beliefs; that you hope this person will abandon homosexual behavior; that you didn't expect to find this out about your loved one, but now, having found it out, you're anxious to know what to do or say, and what *not* to do or say, or both. That's probably why you're reading *When Homosexuality Hits Home*—because now that you know, you have questions.

For nearly 30 years as an ordained pastoral biblical counselor, I've *consulted* with many people who've had questions similar to the ones on your mind now. I've counseled parents reeling from the shock of discovery, wanting to know what, if anything, they did wrong. Or what they can say to change their son's mind, what to do when their daughter wants to bring her lesbian lover home for the holidays, or how to respond when they're called "homophobic" or "bigoted."

Wives too have sat in my office, shattered and bewildered after learning of a husband's sexual secret, wondering if the man she thought she knew was really a stranger she'd never known.

I've wept with grown men whose fathers "came out" later in life, sometimes contracting AIDS in the process and devastating entire families. I've listened to the concerns of family members who've asked how to handle their openly gay sibling's wanting to spend time with their kids, or what their policy should be at family gatherings; still others have asked how to answer the claims of relatives who say they're both gay and Christian.

In each case, I've wished I could put a how-to book into their hands. And so, with that wish in mind, this book was written.

My interest in the subject is more than professional, though. It's deeply personal, because homosexuality hit my own home, long ago, bringing indescribable pain and misunderstanding along with it.

ôô ôô ôô

Sex itself became a source of confusion to me when I was repeatedly molested by pedophiles in my neighborhood—men who were skilled at manipulating boys into sexual favors. These encounters introduced me to pornography, orgies, and a number of other perversions, leaving me jaded and obsessed with sex from an early age. So by the time I was an adolescent, I was involved with adult men, girls, and boys. The sexual revolution of the 1960s was in full swing, and "doing it" seemed to be on everyone's mind. That suited me fine; I indulged whenever I could, and I was oddly proud of the fact that I knew more about sex than most of my friends. I had learned to manipulate and seduce, having been seduced myself, and when I used these skills on girls at my school, I was quick to brag openly about my conquests.

Sex with guys was another matter. I enjoyed it when it happened but never spoke of it, much less bragged about it, to anyone. (As liberal as the times were, the "revolution" only condoned casual sex between men and women; sex between men was still looked down on.) I never considered myself to be completely homosexual, since girls still held a genuine appeal to me. But during drunken high school parties, field trips, or sleepovers with a friend, I always looked for sexual opportunities. They came frequently; more frequently than any of us would have dared to admit. And by the time I was 15, I also added having sex with adult men, whom I would contact through an underground gay dating service, to my list of secret practices.

In a way, it was all exciting and flattering. But questions about my future—*Will I ever outgrow my homosexual tendencies? Will I ever be caught in the act? Will I ever get married?*—all began to pile up, taking an emotional toll. By the time I was in high school, I was often depressed, and when I wasn't acting out sexually, I spent most of my free time alone.

It was during those early high school years that my parents started to comment on my emotional withdrawal. After coming home from school, I'd head straight for my room, where I would remain, door shut and locked, until called for dinner. I'd eat quickly and silently, answering questions about my day with the briefest possible response, then excuse myself at the first opportunity. I refused to watch television with my parents and brothers, preferring the solitude of my own room where I could indulge my private loves of music, reading, and sexual fantasy. The family who loved me became, God forgive me, an unwelcome intrusion into my life.

By my sixteenth birthday, my parents were becoming alarmed. My grades dropped; I was skipping classes to go to the beach alone and sit for hours on the sand, staring into nothingness; and my isolation had worsened. They began asking questions: Was it drugs? Was I depressed? Did I want to talk to a psychiatrist?

How could I tell them—how could *anyone* in 1971 tell his parents—*No, nothing's wrong, I just like to have sex with guys. I'm one of those queers I've heard you make jokes about so many times, Dad. Oh, and Mom, if you remember warning me when I was little to stay away from the downtown theaters because there were men there who might want me, you were right, they wanted me. I lost my virginity eight years ago, and I'm seriously won-dering if I'll ever have anything close to a normal life.*

And therein lay the problem. Isolated as I was from my parents, the last thing I wanted to do was hurt them with the truth. Hurting them with my silence seemed kinder.

The silence was broken the spring I attended a Bible study at Calvary Chapel of Costa Mesa, a Southern California megachurch that was experiencing an electrifying revival known as the Jesus Movement. Thousands of kids—most of them hippie types recently converted to Christianity—went there weekly to worship and to sit under Pastor Chuck Smith's teaching. A strikingly beautiful classmate had asked me to go with her and, in retrospect, I'm sure she sensed some of my inner turmoil and saw me as a young man who was ripe for the good news.

The gospel I heard Chuck preach that night was plain and direct. When he said, "Man is forever hungry for what only God can give him and is doomed to grasp for love any way he can until he finds the real Source of love," I knew I was being described in merciless detail. For the following three months I wrestled with the immensity of conversion, wondering how I could follow Christ and abandon the sexual behavior that by now seemed to define me. But the more I pondered concepts like eternity, God, and death, the more I wondered how I could afford *not* to follow Christ and abandon my sexual behavior. Finally, exhausted from conviction and inner debate, I quietly embraced His promise that anyone who came to Him would not be cast out.

I was born again, and this time I refused to keep my parents excluded from my experience. I needed them to know what had happened to me, if for no other reason than to explain why I was going to start attending church five times a week.

Yet explaining my salvation to them meant, as far as I was concerned, explaining why I needed a Savior. And that meant the unthinkable—telling them everything. Even though I was now committed to abstinence, having decided to put my sexual behaviors behind me, I somehow felt Mom and Dad were entitled to know about my past. It was a faltering, naïve way of trying to bridge the gap. I wanted honesty to be a part of my new life.

So, shortly after the day I was converted, I told them. I told them bluntly, without forewarning, oblivious to the agony it would cause them. I assumed (naïvely—is there any other word for it?) they would be happy I had abandoned homosexuality, fornication, and the use of pornography. It didn't occur to my teenage mind, however good my intentions were, that in telling them I had *abandoned* these behaviors, I was forcing them to deal with my having been *involved* in them in the first place. It meant forcing them to envision their son being sexually abused, then realizing they'd been kept in the dark about the abuse and its effects for years. It meant they'd have to hear that I had committed the sort of sexual acts they considered to be the most abominable, forcing them to wonder if they'd done anything to create such monstrous tendencies in their own son. It meant dragging them through the mud of my perversions—and yet, even as they were being dragged, I expected them to react calmly.

Of course, I was disappointed. Mother collapsed in tears; my father screamed, swore, attacked. The night I told my parents that I'd been involved in homosexuality, my disclosure had the effect of a death sentence. Our family would never be the same.

What we endured that night and for years thereafter—years in which I went into full-time ministry, then backslid into homosexuality and gay activism, years in which I served on staff with a local gay church and preached that homosexuality and Christianity were compatible, then finally, after six years of self-delusion, repented at age 29 and made a new start—all of that has taught me a good deal about what a family can and cannot bear.

I am certain my parents believed, when I first blurted out my confession, that life had ended. In their eyes, I had died; in my eyes, they'd become intolerant, unreasonable enemies. All of us prayed, in our own ways, for God to somehow bring good out of this disaster. But we couldn't foresee a happy ending, not that night nor for years to come. And we would have disbelieved anyone who told us that one day we'd all be laughing and dancing together on my wedding day; that I would become a full-time counselor to families and individuals going through crises similar to ours; or that I would give my parents grandchildren who would honor them and become the delight of their later years. In the midst of our pain and rage, such happy wishes, though all of them would eventually come true, were simply unthinkable.

→→→   →→→   →→→

Now, the details of your situation may be different. But I'll bet your family and mine have a lot in common, so please believe me when I say I've been there. That too is why this book was written.

I'll admit, reluctantly, that it's also written out of anger—not the noblest of motives, but a strong one. Being a Christian consultant (or "life coach," as we're often called) who counsels from a biblical perspective, I know that when a loved one comes out as gay, the right response is not to condone homosexuality, nor is it to despise the homosexual person. But I've been seeing both these extremes—the whitewashing of the sin, or the cruel mistreatment of the sinner—practiced by too many people for too many years. And it's the family members who are so often miserably caught in the middle.

Take, for example, the parents who came to me after they were told by their pastor that they should cut off all communication with their adult gay son. When they argued, "But we love him," the pastor retorted, "As long as you associate with him, you're loving him straight to hell!" They wondered if their only option as Christians was to reject their son entirely.

I also recall a mother who was warned by a school counselor that her refusal to allow her teenage son to join an on-campus gay support group would increase the likelihood of his committing suicide. She was further told that Bible-based beliefs such as hers were the cause of depression and suicide among gay teenagers and that she was directly responsible for creating a climate that encouraged people to assault and murder homosexuals. Her choice? According to the counselor, it was "Hold on to your beliefs and kill your son, or become a better mother by discarding your beliefs."

And during a conference I attended years ago, the wives in the audience were told by the featured speaker that if their husbands were homosexual, they should love them unconditionally by saying nothing about their sin. In fact, this speaker encouraged each woman to continue having sex with her gay husband—even if he was promiscuous and it meant running the risk of HIV infection—because that was the Christlike thing to do.

Whole chapters could be devoted to similar examples, each story as heartbreaking and senseless as the ones I've described. So each year, with every new story, I found myself increasingly angry over the pain inflicted on so many families who've been impacted by homosexuality.

It's also irritating to see pro-gay television shows, movies, and plays multiply while there are so few resources written from a Christian perspective available to help people with gay loved ones. And while I'm venting, let me point out the mean-spiritedness so many people, both Christian and non-Christian, display toward homosexuals and, on the other extreme, the astonishing, blasphemous compromises a number of churches and denominations are making as they embrace homosexuality and reject biblical authority.

᙮᙮   ᙮᙮   ᙮᙮

However, unless anger gets converted into something redemptive, it's useless. And so I want this book, inspired at least partly by anger, to be a practical resource for you. It's written with three primary goals in mind:

First, I want to help you better understand your gay loved one by better understanding his or her experience, both past and present. To understand a person does not mean you agree; rather, it helps you to better communicate and relate with that person.

Second, I hope it will help you preserve your relationship without compromising your own beliefs about homosexuality. This will require some negotiating, some boundary setting, and a good deal of mutual respect and patience. I find this to be the greatest challenge when homosexuality hits home, and in this book we'll learn to rise and meet it.

Finally, this is written to help you articulate the biblical position on homosexuality, since there's more than a good chance you'll be discussing this issue for some time. This book will lay out many of the common pro-gay arguments you're likely to encounter and will help you develop responses to each.

In other words, I hope this will be the sort of guidebook my family and I wished we'd had when we were facing these challenges.

To meet these goals, I've tried to cover most of, if not all, the different situations families of homosexual loved ones find themselves in. Specifically, the chapters will address

- parents with a gay adult son or daughter
- parents with a gay teenage son or daughter
- spouses who discover a partner is homosexual
- brothers or sisters with a gay or lesbian sibling
- people who have a gay extended-family member (for example, uncle, in-law)

You'll probably find yourself in one of these chapters. But if you are personally struggling with homosexuality, let me recommend my first book, *Desires in Conflict* (Harvest House, 2003), or if you're struggling with lesbianism, Anne Paulk's book *Restoring Sexual Identity* (Harvest House, 2003). Both are written directly to the person wanting to overcome homosexuality and will no doubt be more helpful to you than this book, which is written for a different audience.

If you're part of this audience, know that I've tried to make this book as user-friendly as possible. While some chapters are general, others specifically address different types of family relationships—so you can go straight to the chapter that applies to you and your situation without reading the other situation-specific chapters, which may not be of interest to you.

To get you started, let me suggest you read chapters 1 and 2, which will apply to anyone with a homosexual family member. Then go straight to the chapter that concerns you, which will be the chapter for parents (chapter 3); for parents of teens who say they're gay (chapter 4); for spouses (chapter 5); or for other family members (chapter 6).

Some paragraphs in chapters 3 through 6 overlap, so if you read all of them, you'll notice identical or nearly identical paragraphs in some sections. That's because some of the specific steps and advice I would give to parents may be the same steps or advice I'd offer to spouses or extended-family members. So while each chapter has its own focus, you'll also find certain points repeated in each. That's not due to laziness on my part but, rather, is because some of these points apply to all family members and need to be included in all chapters.

After reading the chapter pertaining to you and your situation, move on to chapter 7, "Negotiating Family Boundaries," which will, I hope, be of practical use to all readers. In fact, a desire to help families negotiate boundaries was one of my primary goals in writing this book.

Chapter 8 addresses a specific boundary, one dealing with a situation that's more and more common—an invitation to a same-sex wedding.

Chapter 9 addresses three of the most common pro-gay arguments ("I was born this way," "you're homophobic," and "gay marriage is valid") and provides examples of the sorts of conversations you'll probably have with your gay family member, including arguments or questions he or she is likely to pose and biblical and commonsense answers you can respond with. They're offered to prepare you for these discussions and are apologetic in nature. That, I think, is fitting. Homosexuality is one of the primary hot-button issues of our time, and the church has a mandate to speak to current issues. So if we want to be relevant—to our loved ones, associates, and the culture at large—we'd better be prepared to answer pro-gay claims and questions; first by understanding them, then by responding to them clearly and lovingly.

Chapter 10 adds to chapter 9 by providing additional talking points. If, as you hope, you are able to maintain a connection with your loved one, you will likely have chances for ongoing discussion of beliefs, lifestyles, and choices. This chapter helps prepare you to be both truthful and loving.

Finally, chapter 11, "A Mile in Their Shoes," will provide, I hope, an opportunity to better understand what life has been like for your gay family member. Seeing his or her side of this debate is essential if we want to be compassionate, caring people. And the best way I know of seeing someone else's side is by attempting to better understand that person's life experience. So I hope you'll take time to read this chapter as well, and read it carefully.

Now, a few words about the terms for homosexual people that will be used in these chapters, especially the term *gay:*

I'm aware of the objections some Christians have to using the word *gay* when describing a homosexual. In fact, I've been called on the carpet more than once for using this term when addressing churches or leading seminars, since many people think the word *gay* should be reserved strictly for references to happiness, not to homosexuals.

To a point, I understand and agree. The term *gay* has been co-opted by the gay-rights movement to the point that you can hardly sing, "Don we now our gay apparel" without snickering. So I sympathize with those who think we should limit ourselves to the word *homosexual* when describing people attracted to the same sex. But for the writer or speaker, this presents the problem of redundancy. Since homosexuals have to be referred to frequently in these pages, it will become monotonous if I keep using the same ten-letter word every few sentences. So please bear with me as I use the terms *homosexual, gay, lesbian,* or *lesbian and gay* interchangeably. In doing so, I'm not trying to make a political statement. I'm just trying to keep us both from becoming bored. Also, I may sometimes use the generic pronoun *he* or *she* alone rather than the perhaps more politically correct *he or she.* Be assured that most of the statements apply to either gender.

Let's begin, then, to address what to do and say when homosexuality hits home. And as we begin, let's remember one of the most remarkable descriptions of Jesus we find in the gospels:

> The Word became flesh and dwelt among us, and we beheld
> His glory, the glory as of the only begotten of the Father, full
> of grace and truth (John 1:14).

Grace and truth—the enormous challenge to be honest and loving; firm in our convictions and unsparing in our compassion; as clear in our beliefs as we are generous in our love. When someone you love is gay, you become more aware than ever of your inability to face life's challenges apart from the grace of God.

So as we seek a Christlike response to our gay family members, may what was said of Him be said of us as well—that we are, as He was, full of grace and truth.

Chapter 1

Now That You Know

*Flashing in my mind was this wonderful son
who was so bubbly and happy—such a joy to have
around. Thinking of him entwined with some other
male brought heaves of heavy
sobbing from deep wounds of agony.*

—Barbara Johnson
Where Does a Mother Go to Resign?

The closer you are, the more it hurts. So if a casual friend or co-worker is gay, you're probably concerned, but not devastated. It's another matter if you've learned this about a daughter, son, spouse, or immediate family member. At first you may have refused to believe it. Maybe you hoped "I'm gay" really meant "I'm confused," or "I'm going through a phase." Then finally, for whatever reason, it sinks in: *This person I love is a homosexual.*

That's when the emotional roller coaster takes off, and you can expect to experience every feeling imaginable while you're riding it. But now that you know—before we examine the ups and downs you'll experience—let's begin with an understanding that you're not alone in this. Countless parents, spouses, family members, and friends have been there too. And wherever they may stand on the morality of homosexuality, they would, I'm sure, confirm how difficult it can be when a loved one announces, "I'm gay."

When Cher (*the* Cher) first heard those words from her daughter, Chastity, she threw her out of the home. Barbra Streisand had an easier time accepting her son's homosexuality, but his recent admission of being infected with the AIDS virus has to have been crushing. Liza Minelli found out about her first husband's homosexuality by walking in on him while he was in the middle of an encounter with a man. In this she shares her mother, Judy Garland's, misfortune: Garland was married, not once but twice, to men who were later found to be homosexual. Comedienne Joan Rivers was spared a similar fate by discovering her boyfriend's homosexuality before marrying him, a discovery she initially, like many women, refused to accept.

Actress Lana Turner assumed she'd done something wrong as a mother when her daughter Cheryl admitted her lesbianism, and Dr. Charles Socarides, a nationally recognized psychologist who has pioneered and promoted clinical treatment for homosexuals, is himself the father of a gay son.

Christians and social conservatives aren't exempt from this experience, either. Former speaker of the house Newt Gingrich has been challenged publicly more than once by his lesbian half-sister, who opposes many of his conservative views. Former vice president Dick Cheney has a smoother relationship with his lesbian daughter, although he clearly does not condone lesbianism, and the late senator Pete Knight of California, who authored a ballot proposition designed to prevent state recognition of same-sex marriages, had both a homosexual brother and son.

At least three of today's top-selling Christian authors also know a bit of what you're going through. Philip Yancey has written extensively about his friendship with gay activist Mel White and the tensions White's "coming out" created for them both, in *What's So Amazing About Grace?* In *How Will I Tell My Mother?* Stephen Arterburn chronicles his gay brother's battle with AIDS and his family's response. And popular author and speaker the late Barbara Johnson describes her family's shock over her son's homosexuality in her first book, *Where Does a Mother Go to Resign?*

Additionally, the son of pro-family activist Phyllis Schlafly admitted years ago to being gay, and televangelist Oral Roberts endured the worst sort of tragedy when his homosexual son committed suicide in 1981.

Clearly, then, you're not alone—not in the discovery that someone you love is gay nor in the heartache coming after the discovery. You have lots of company, which, some say, misery loves. But company alone can't take away your pain, so let's examine that pain and, hopefully, learn how best to handle it.

"It Feels Like He Died"

When listening to people describe their feelings about a homosexual loved one, *death* is the word I hear most often. Of course, words like *shock, fear,* and *confusion* are used as well, but the phrase "it feels like he died" comes up more than any other.

Sometimes literal death is referred to in these conversations, as in "I'm so miserable I wish I could die," "I'm so scared he'll die of AIDS," or "If she continues in this, she'll die spiritually, once and for all." Other times, the word is used more figuratively: "I'll just die if any of my friends find out," or "His father will die when he hears this."

When homosexuality hits home, I've come to believe that there *is* a death involved, though it's not the death of the gay individual or of his relations with his family. But it's the death of *assumptions*.

Every relationship is based on assumptions. We assume the person we're in relationship with is someone we know pretty well, so we trust there are no major secrets between us. We assume this individual tells us the truth and shares our values, and that our relationship will go on in a fairly predictable way.

We hold even more specific assumptions based on the sort of relationship we have. If we're married, we assume our spouses are and will continue to be faithful; that they will always be our partners; that we are *safe* in our marriages. If we're parents, we assume our daughter or son will live out the principles we've taught in the home and that we'll become grandparents someday. If we have brothers or sisters, we assume each will eventually develop a traditional family unit of their own and give us nieces and nephews.

And in most cases, since homosexuality is more the exception than the rule, we assume our loved one is heterosexual.

To hear otherwise, then, signals the death of assumptions. Suddenly, we find we *don't* know our loved one as well as we thought. We realize he or she has had a secret problem—a secret *life*, perhaps—that we've known nothing about. We may have been lied to, directly or indirectly, shattering the assumption that our relationship was founded on honesty. Our loved one may not, we learn, share our values, and our future with this person is now anything but predictable.

Our assumption of monogamy may die—a spouse has found another partner in fantasy or real life, and how can we compete? Or the assumption our son or daughter will carry on our tradition, both religious and relational, expires when we learn our child has feelings we never assumed he or she would feel, and now holds beliefs we never imagined a member of our family would hold.

So many assumptions, all lost. It's neither morbid nor inaccurate to call it death. So clarify these points to yourself:

- Your loved one did *not* die.

- Your *relationship* with this person hasn't died either. It will take time and effort to rebuild, perhaps, but there's no reason to assume the bonds between the two of you are severed.

- You *are* experiencing the death of assumptions, and major assumptions at that. So in response to this death, as in response to death of any sort, you're grieving.

Your Loss and the Stages of Grief

More than 30 years ago, Dr. Elisabeth Kübler-Ross developed a theory on the stages of grief we experience when someone close to us dies. While she clearly does not write from a Christian perspective, Dr. Kübler-Ross's ideas about death and dying are useful. She breaks grief into five general stages or phases: denial, anger, bargaining, depression, and acceptance. Anyone who has worked with grieving families will tell you this progression of five stages accurately describes the emotional process they go through.

But many people, including me, believe these phases are common to people experiencing loss or death of any sort: the loss or death of a job, a marriage, or in your case, *assumptions*. Faced with this loss, family members who've just learned about a loved one's homosexuality can expect to experience stages of grief similar to those Dr. Kübler-Ross describes. Let's look at each so we can get a better understanding of what you're likely to go through.

Denial: "He can't be gay!"

When Barbara Johnson discovered gay pornography in her son's desk drawer, she decided it must be part of a homework assignment he was working on. Lesbian activist Robin Tyler's mother heard a rumor her daughter was a "dyke," so Ms. Tyler assured her mom that *dyke* was slang for "Doctor of Young Karate Experts." And time and again, when parents or family members have called my office to inquire about their homosexual loved one, they begin the conversation by asking, "Can you help my family member? He's confused. He *thinks* he's gay."

"How long," I ask, "has he thought that?"

"Ten, maybe twelve, years."

He's not confused; Mrs. Johnson's son wasn't doing research; and *dyke,* while a crude word, was at least accurate and had nothing to do with karate. In each case, homosexuality had hit home long before the home was willing to admit it.

That's understandable. Denial kicks in when we're confronted with something unacceptable, something wildly contrary to our expectations and dreams.

I remember, for example, getting a phone call from my father in the fall of 1987. As usual, he was brief and to the point: He had a malignancy in his throat; he would begin treatment shortly; it didn't look good; and he wanted me to be prepared.

Unacceptable. Absolutely not. No way. After all, I'd just been married that summer, and Dad had kicked up his heels like a schoolboy at the reception, beaming and rejoicing with me and my bride. We'd been through so much by then—so many exhausting arguments, so much hostility—all buried when I recommitted myself to Christ after years of gay activism, then went through intensive therapy, immense personal changes and, finally, engagement to my beautiful wife, Renee. Dad and I were getting close for the first time; the worst was behind us. I was sure he would live to see my career take off, enjoy my children, and have a full, peaceful retirement. That *had* to happen.

So of course I didn't believe him. I heard the words "I have cancer," but they didn't register. Even as I hung up the phone after assuring him of my love and prayers, I said out loud, "Nope. It's not cancer; it's not malignant; he's not dying." Then I went about my business as though nothing had happened, holding out hope that what I'd just been told meant something else—anything else—than what I was refusing to face.

Who could blame me? And who, for that matter, can blame you? When you love, you invest in expectations. So think for a moment of all you've expected to happen in your loved one's life, then consider how the news "I'm gay" has affected those expectations. Certain things were supposed to happen—to your thinking, they probably *had* to happen—so you heard the words and, like me, told yourself they meant something else.

Considering all we hope and wish for the people we love, it's no wonder that, when we're confronted with bad news about them, we refuse to believe it. So your emotions will probably not fully register what your ears have already taken in—not at first. That's denial, the initial stage of the grief process. It doesn't mean there's anything wrong with you. It just means you, like all of us, are slow to accept the unacceptable.

If this is where you are...then don't criticize yourself for finding it hard to believe someone you love is gay. No one lets go of assumptions easily. It takes time.

On the other hand, just because you're reluctant to believe your loved one is gay, don't force your denial on him by saying, in effect, "Since *I* can't believe you're homosexual, therefore you *can't* be homosexual!" At least give the person credit for thinking this through. After all, long before he decided to come out to you with this news he thought it over carefully. So if your loved one has made this announcement to you, take it at face value. If she said, "I'm lesbian" or he said, "I'm gay," don't retort, "No, you're not!" just because *you* find it hard to believe. Instead, let this person know it's hard for you to believe this and you'll need time before it really sinks in.

It should also be said, though, that in some cases a person really *doesn't* know for certain whether or not he's gay. Sometimes a homosexual relationship is just an experiment and nothing more; sometimes gay pornography is looked at just out of curiosity. And at times, people can be confused about their sexual orientation, leading them to draw premature conclusions. So while I consider it a mistake to try to tell someone what they are or aren't feeling, I also see value in asking a few simple questions at this point:

"How do you know if you're really homosexual?"

"How long have you felt this way?"

"How much do you know about homosexuality?"

The answers to these questions won't solve the problem, of course. They may be very hard to hear, in fact. But they'll at least help you determine whether your reluctance to believe your loved one is gay stems from confusion on his part or from denial on yours. If it's denial, it will dissolve, probably soon, giving way to the next common stage of the grief process.

Anger: "He's gay—I'll kill him!"

When it sinks in that the unthinkable is true, anger is a common response.

I'm sure you remember where you were on September 11, 2001, when you first heard about the terrorist attacks on the World Trade Center and the Pentagon. Remember the initial shock of looking at television images that seemed so unreal? Even as the facts were reported in detail over the news channels, most of us couldn't grasp them. It was too much of a catastrophe; too horrible, completely unbelievable.

But of course we had no choice but to believe it, so after the truth sank in, the outrage began. Likewise, on a much smaller scale, outrage begins when you realize your own home or private life has been disrupted by something you never anticipated.

This can be the most destructive of all the grief stages, so for the sake of everyone involved, be careful how you react. When you're angry, you may want the relief of an emotional explosion, and that may cause you to use the harshest, deadliest words you can think of. I've known parents who, out of their own rage, told their sons or daughters they'd rather see them dead than gay. I've heard brothers call a homosexual sibling a "freak who oughta be strung up and burned" (I'm quoting exact words here!), and I've seen whole families reject and humiliate a gay relative through name-calling and cruel, senseless remarks. And in each case, these family members lived to regret—bitterly—every vicious word they spit out at their loved ones but couldn't retract or erase, as much as they wanted to.

So again, be careful. There's nothing wrong with anger, but a great deal of wrong comes from misusing it. "Be angry," Paul told the Ephesians, "and do not sin" (Ephesians 4:26). There's the challenge.

Properly used, anger can help correct a problem. Some of the finest social movements in history were birthed because people got collectively angry over an injustice, angry enough to do something about it. In counseling, I've seen anger provide a man with the motivation he needs to finally confront a problem. And no one can deny the value of Jesus' anger when he threw the money changers out of the temple. Anger, properly used, motivates us to recognize a problem and correct it.

Wrath, though, corrects nothing. Instead, it lashes out, damaging and destroying. That's why James said, "The wrath of man does not produce the righteousness of God" (James 1:20). Screaming threats and insults at a family member doesn't help your situation. It does a lot to wound the person you love and to cripple any ability to ever trust you again, but it does nothing to solve or improve the situation at hand. And regardless of any relief you temporarily get from blowing off steam, in the end your explosion will have made everything much, much worse.

The trick, then, is to determine whether your anger is legitimate and then to express it constructively.

A few examples of legitimate anger and constructive expression versus expression of wrath might be as follows:

- *When a married man has committed adultery with another man.*

  - His wife is legitimately angry for having been lied to, betrayed, and maybe physically endangered by a sexually transmitted disease.

  - Constructive expression: "You lied to me and broke your vows—who knows, you might even have infected me! Of course I'm furious!"

  - Expression of wrath: "You're a worthless whoremonger who doesn't give a rip about anybody!"

- *When a son has been using gay pornography in his parents' home, knowing how strongly they would object to porn in any form.*
    - His parents are legitimately angry over his lack of consideration for them, their home, and their values.
    - Constructive expression: "You brought things into our home that you knew we'd never allow. You've completely disrespected us and our right to decide what comes into our house!"
    - Expression of wrath: "You make me sick! Anyone who wants to look at this stuff is disgusting. You're disgusting!"

- *When a man marries a woman without telling her about his homosexual attractions.*
    - The wife who discovers this is legitimately angry over having been misled.
    - Constructive expression: "You let me believe one thing when you knew, and deliberately covered up, that you're turned on by men. You had no right!"
    - Expression of wrath: "Our marriage is a joke, and you're a pervert who's used me!"

- *When a daughter takes financial support from her parents, including money for rent, while telling them she lives alone or has a roommate when in fact she's in a lesbian relationship.*
    - The parents are legitimately angry over her willingness to accept their support under false pretenses.
    - Constructive expression: "You manipulated us, lied to us, used us!"
    - Expression of wrath: "You and your perverted little friend can burn for all we care!"

- *When a man demands that his family recognize his relationship with another man as a marriage, threatening to cut them off if they don't.*
  - The family is legitimately angry over his stridency and heavy-handedness.
  - Constructive expression: "You're acting like royalty, throwing out demands and ultimatums. There's going to have to be some compromise here!"
  - Expression of wrath: "Take your stupid gay-rights parade someplace else!"

In each case, you'll notice the people involved aren't angry just because their loved one is homosexual. They're angry over the way that person has handled, or mishandled, the relationship. The constructive expressions, you'll also notice, are angry without being insulting or sarcastic, whereas the expressions of wrath aren't meant to correct the problem as much as they're intended to hurt the individual. And that's where the difference is crucial.

If this is where you are…then stop and think about how you've handled your anger. Of course you're mad—someone you love has embraced a sin that's going to disrupt life as you know it and, whether he realizes it or not, estrange him from God. How could you be anything but angry?

So if you spoke your piece without insulting, threatening, or degrading your loved one; if you let him know how you felt without attacking him or calling him names; if you can look back on what you said when you found out he was gay without regretting your words or your tone—then congratulations. You've been angry without sinning.

But if at this point you realize your words were harsh or poorly chosen; if out of your own pain you said things you didn't mean; if you injured someone you love with a verbal assault—and I'm sure you know what qualifies as "assault"—then you have your own sin to deal with. After all, it makes no sense to criticize a homosexual for doing something the Bible condemns when you disobey the same Bible, which commands you to "let your speech always be with grace, seasoned with salt" (Colossians 4:6).

So go to him or her and apologize. Explain that, although you're grieved and angry over his or her sin, you now realize you've also sinned, both in attitude and words. Ask forgiveness. Let your loved one know you're still not sure how the two of you are going to work out your relationship, but that you want to preserve it even if you can't agree on this issue. And emphasize that you want your discussions, no matter how heated, to be respectful.

There's a good chance you'll still be angry, not just with your gay loved one but also at the darker aspects of life in general—sin, Satan, this fallen world. All of these are legitimate reasons for anger, but remember the difference between anger and wrath. Anger, properly used, exposes a sin and tries to correct it, whereas wrath only seeks to hurt.

Anger is a scalpel; wrath is an ax. Before you pick up either one, be sure you know how you intend to use it.

And be sure you can live with the results.

Bargaining: "He's gay. So now what?"

Dr. Kübler-Ross describes this phase as being somewhat irrational, a time when the grieving person tries to bargain with God.

I've been there. Once I'd finished railing at God for allowing my father's cancer, I then tried striking deals with Him. "If Dad watches his diet and we get him the best nursing care," I prayed, "then maybe You could tag a few extra years onto his life. Deal?"

Similarly, it's common for the terminally ill to make promises in hopes of a reprieve. ("God, let me live and I'll quit smoking," or "Heal my heart and I swear I'll lose weight!") That, Kübler-Ross says, is the bargaining phase.

But there's a more constructive, realistic form of bargaining we can engage in. It begins when we and our gay family member have reached the point where we realize all the fighting on earth won't change anything. He's still who he is; we're still who we are. Neither of us is going to budge. Now what?

That's when we move beyond our anger and start asking the hard but practical questions, such as these:

> "Okay, we disagree on homosexuality, so should we drop the topic or keep discussing it?"
>
> "Are you expecting me to welcome your partner into our home?"
>
> "I teach my kids that sex is only moral and normal when it's between a husband and wife. Even if you disagree, can you respect that when you're in my home?"

All these can be summed up in one general question: "Under what terms are we going to continue to have a relationship?"

Whatever answers you come to, you'll probably arrive at them through *negotiation*. And that's what makes this the most constructive part of the grieving process.

When you negotiate, or bargain, you set the terms of your relationship through discussion and mutual agreement. Both you and your loved one will still have some pretty deep feelings at this point. You both may still be angry or deeply hurt, but when you negotiate, you're going to let reason, not emotion, guide the discussion. And reason tells you that in this relationship, as in all relationships, some things are negotiable and some are not. So start with the nonnegotiables—that is, the terms or boundaries that you're *not* willing to change. Here's a list of some common nonnegotiables:

> "My *position* is nonnegotiable. I'll never say I approve of homosexuality or that I agree with you when in fact I don't."

"*Mutual respect* is nonnegotiable. I won't be insulted or demeaned for holding my beliefs, no matter how strongly you disagree with them."

"The *standards in my home* are nonnegotiable. I won't allow any open display of homosexuality or materials I feel are inappropriate in my house."

"Your *free will* is God-given and nonnegotiable. I'll respect it and your right to make your own decisions, even when we disagree." (Note: If your loved one is a minor, there will be limits to this, which we'll discuss in chapters 3 and 4.)

"I'll always love and value you, no matter how differently we see things. And that love is definitely and eternally nonnegotiable."

These nonnegotiables still leave plenty of room for you and your loved one to decide what *is* negotiable. In deciding how to set terms with people, the apostle Paul encourages us,

> If it is possible, as much as depends on you, live peaceably with all men (Romans 12:18).

Notice he did not say, "Agree with all men, or force all men to agree with you." Nor did he say, "No matter what, live peaceably with all men, even if they make outrageous demands on you." His words are reasonable: As much as possible, with believers and nonbelievers alike, we should try to maintain peaceful relations. And peace often requires negotiation, or naming the "negotiables."

In the following chapters, we'll look at some common "negotiable points" that are likely to come up, and we'll go into the how-to's of negotiation in more detail. For now, I only want you to understand the *essence* of this part of the process. This is the time for you and the person you love to sit down and discuss under what terms you're going to continue to relate. And you will, I hope, discuss this with the understanding that you want to preserve the relationship as much as possible, because in all but the most extreme cases, it's not just possible—it's advisable.

If this is where you are...then let your family member know that you want to protect what the two of you already have. You have history, shared memories, affection, and any number of experiences that have bonded you. Tell your loved one you value what you have and you're setting the terms of your relationship so you can preserve it. That's what boundaries and terms are for: preserving the relationship.

Do be honest and realistic about this. Now that you know your loved one is gay, things can't be the same. You grieve over the sin; he grieves over your inability to call it anything but sin. But just because things can't be the same doesn't mean they can't be *good.* They can, but how good they're going to be depends largely on how well the two of you negotiate.

So think over your terms. Start with the nonnegotiables. Prayerfully list them and make sure they are in fact nonnegotiable. Then sit down for a heart-to-heart with your family member. Show him your nonnegotiables, ask what his are as well, then hash out the negotiables. A good way to begin is by asking, "How do you want us to relate to each other from now on? What do you want from me, and what do you want our relationship to be like?"

Those questions, asked honestly, can be the starting point for constructive negotiation. And negotiation will help protect the bond you and your gay loved one have had.

Depression: "He's gay; I'm miserable."

My father died in the early hours of an April morning in 1988. When my older brother called me with the news, I'd already been through denial, raged my way through anger, and struck as many bargains with God as I could muster. Now it was over, and I was appointed executor of Dad's estate. That meant a whole slew of responsibilities had just been dropped on me, so as soon as I hung up the phone, I kicked into a sort of emotional autopilot. There were papers to file, people to contact, courts to visit, bills to pay. In short, there was so much to *do,* there was no time to *feel.*

Until there was finally nothing more to do. When the estate closed and the administrative work was over, then and only then did the full weight of my loss sink in. Tears started coming at the most unexpected times; waves of sadness would hit, dreams about Dad would come and go, and my energy went down to the point that, at times, I couldn't seem to do the simplest tasks. That's when I learned to respect the word *depression.*

After you've talked through all the terms and boundaries, had all the arguments, and hashed out all your differences with your gay loved one, you realize there's nothing more to do. Except, perhaps, to weep. And that is probably when the full weight of your situation is going to settle in, and you'll begin the depression phase.

Anyone who says you just have to snap out of it knows little or nothing about true depression. When you're depressed, you're not just sad; you're *overwhelmed.* This is especially true when love—that wonderful something that's supposed to make life worthwhile—has now become a source of agony. You love someone, and the someone you love is in sin. Serious sin. Worse, you're helpless. You can't change your loved one's mind, nor can you change your love. So now love means pain—the pain of worrying, wondering, grieving. It's a pain that frequently evolves into depression.

When depression hits, you feel as though you're walking through Jell-O. Every move, even the slightest routine activity, seems like a marathon. You tend to oversleep or not sleep at all. You either lose your appetite entirely or you overeat, finding food the only source of comfort left in your life. Your attitude becomes pessimistic in the extreme; you see no hope or future. Your energy is gone, your interests are limited, and you withdraw from everyone. That's depression, and calling it "hell" doesn't seem extreme.

Barbara Johnson describes lying in bed, listless and sobbing, worrying day and night about her gay son. She likened her depression to an elephant standing on top of her chest, an apt illustration to anyone who's been there. It's a vile combination of misery, loss, and utter hopelessness, and it's one of life's worst experiences. No one is exempt from it, not even the godliest and strongest. The prophet Elijah expressed it well when he was exhausted and discouraged, fleeing for his life from Jezebel and, according to 1 Kings 19:4, "he prayed that he might die."

"It is enough," he lamented. "Now, LORD, take my life, for I am no better than my fathers!" The man of God, who had recently challenged Baal's prophets and called fire down on the heathen, was radically, inarguably depressed. It can happen to anyone.

If this is where you are...then slow down immediately and don't ask too much of yourself. By "slow down" I mean just that, literally. After all, if someone you loved had died, you'd give yourself time to rest and grieve. And though your gay loved one has not (thank God!) died, your assumptions and hopes for that person have, and that can be devastating. So now's the time to shift your attention away from your gay loved one and turn it toward properly caring for yourself during this season of grief.

Don't misunderstand. I'm all for doing what we can to improve a situation, provided improvement is within our power. But when we've said and done all we can—when we've argued, negotiated, pleaded, wept, and raged—our situation may still remain unchanged. That's the time to turn away from trying to change it and turn toward better equipping ourselves to live successfully (and yes, even *victoriously*) in spite of our circumstances.

When my clients are facing unchangeable circumstances, I encourage them to invest more heavily in what I consider to be three pillars of successful living: the *devotional, relational,* and *recreational* parts of our lives.

The *devotional* pillar is made up of the time we spend reading Scripture, praying, and meditating. These core activities are crucial to any serious Christian, yet I find they're often the first good habits we drop when life gets complicated. I've come to believe, in fact, that lack of regular prayer and Bible study have left millions of Christians malnourished and ill-equipped to deal with the pressures and temptations life throws at them. As believers in Christ, they may have *relationships* with God, but little or no real *intimacy* with Him. And all because they've neglected their devotional lives.

Personal heartbreak throws an uncompromising light on the state of our intimacy with God. It either makes us glad we have it or hunger for it if we don't. And it's certain that, if we don't have devotional lives, we can't sustain ongoing closeness to God. After all, no relationship thrives without listening and speaking to the other person, and it's through reading the Bible that we hear from God and through prayer that we speak to Him, and He to us.

So we have to draw closer to Him by investing daily in both. And when we do, we're built up spiritually, our love for Him increases, and we're better able to face our circumstances with a level of trust and peace we wouldn't otherwise have.

When my younger son, Jeremy, was five, a citywide power blackout hit our home. He and I were on opposite ends of the house, and since it was already dark outside when our lights went out, the inside of the house was suddenly black as ink. Immediately, I heard my frightened boy yell "Daddy!" from his upstairs bedroom, so I scrambled up to where he was, hoisted him onto my back, and said, "Hop up and grab on." He was vulnerable and confused, and it was so dark he had no idea how to get from one end of the house to the other.

But he didn't need to know. His only job was to stay close to me, and I'd get him where he needed to go.

When homosexuality hits home, you may be vulnerable and confused, having no idea how to get from one point to the next. That's when
God says, "Hop up and grab on." Your job is not to figure out how or
when the situation will change. Rather, it's to draw close to Him and let
Him get you where you need to be. So recommit yourself now to the
daily routine of reading at least one chapter of the Bible and spending a
regularly scheduled amount of time in prayer. Do this, and your closeness to Him can't help but grow, and your ability to walk through this
difficult time can't help but improve.

Depression also throws light on the *relational* pillar of your life and
to what extent you may need to build it up. If you're depressed, you
need human contact more than ever. A devotional life will boost your
intimacy with God, which is crucial, but intimacy with God was never
meant to replace human bonds. Humanity was created with specific and
ongoing relational needs; you're no exception. And depression makes
those needs more keenly felt.

I hope you will make good use of your primary relationships (family
members or close friends you can confide in) at this point, because those
closest to you can become lifesavers during hard, depressing times. But
it's also true that sometimes those closest to us, through no fault of their
own, may be unequipped to help. They may not understand our specific
problem, or they themselves may be too overwhelmed to help us deal
with it. (A mother, for example, who's depressed over her son's homosexuality may find that her husband is so overwhelmed with his own pain
that he has little comfort to offer her.) Or for whatever reason, you may
not feel ready to let others know you have a gay or lesbian loved one. So
another sort of relationship I want you to consider at this point is one
that provides specialized support.

When my wife's father died, my mother-in-law's church immediately
sent a bereavement counselor to speak with her. That provided her with
specialized support—that is, support and guidance from someone who

knew what she was going through and could help her understand what bereavement was going to be like. That person offered advice on how she could best manage her life while she was in grief, and gave her some practical "what to do and what not to do" tips. I was impressed by how clearly her church understood her need for empathetic, well-informed counsel.

You could probably use some of that too. You can find it either through your pastor or a professional Christian counselor or a local support group.

Now would be a good time to make an appointment with your pastor, explain your situation to him, and ask if he can offer you some guidance. Or if you prefer, you might get a referral, either from your pastor or a trusted friend, to a professional Christian counselor who treats depression. And you may find immeasurable support and comfort by meeting with a group of parents or family members who are experiencing many of the emotions and conflicts you're going through now. (Names of these can be found in "What to Do Now," the resource section at the back of this book.) All three of these relationships—pastoral, professional, and group—would qualify as specialized support from people who can provide understanding and guidance.

That brings us to *recreation*, the third pillar. This is something often neglected because recreation can seem almost trivial—a luxury you enjoy but can do without.

Only you can't. Think of the word itself—*recreation*—as "re-creating." In essence, that's what it does. When you relax and engage in something you truly enjoy, you recharge yourself. Your mind is refreshed, your feelings are soothed, and your attitude is calmer and more optimistic. In short, you re-create the emotional and mental energy you need to sustain your life. That's the value of recreation, and it's anything but trivial.

Time and again, I've found that my depressed clients have neglected the value of play. Their lives tend to be all about serious matters: work, finances, parenting, church responsibilities. These are the things they plan for and pay attention to, as well they should. But trouble starts when they forget to reserve time for play and fun as well, making their lives one set of tasks after another. Eventually, they start to sag under the weight of these serious matters, drained of mental and emotional reserves because they haven't taken the time to recharge through recreation.

Of course, what's recreational to one person is drudgery to another, as any married couple will testify. So at this point your task is to determine what would be truly soothing, playful and, in general, pleasurable to you. If you're grieving, you may not be up to the more strenuous recreation of a football game or bicycling. No matter. What's necessary is that you engage in some activity you can genuinely enjoy and look forward to on a regular basis. That's one of the most practical and effortless tools I can suggest to a depressed person.

Only you can determine what qualifies as recreation, but whatever it is, it should be something that brings you genuine pleasure, something you look forward to doing, and something that leaves you feeling refreshed and soothed when completed. Within those guidelines, start planning weekly recreation periods and consider them part of your recovery prescription. Because, believe it or not, they are.

Depression, in my experience, tends to last longer than the first three stages of grief. The bad news is, no one can say how long it will last, and when you're in it, it seems eternal. But the good news is, it will fade more quickly when you take some of the steps I've mentioned here. And of course it will go away more quickly when you don't try to force it to do so.

You'll know your depression is fading when you wake up feeling optimistic for no particular reason, or when you find yourself laughing out loud more often, or when your appetite, sleep habits, and energy levels stabilize. That's when your situation will stop seeming insurmountable or impossible. Hard, yes, and certainly not pleasant. But it no longer seems hopeless, and you no longer feel helpless.

All of which means you're getting better, and you're stepping into the final phase of the grief cycle.

Acceptance: "He's gay, I love him, life can still be good."

Look at Paul's second letter to Timothy, and you'll see a portrait of a man who's rightfully disappointed in life and people but has come to a place of acceptance nonetheless. In some of his other epistles, Paul makes it clear he expects hardship, even persecution, as part and parcel of an apostle's life. In fact, by the time he wrote this letter to Timothy, he'd been imprisoned for preaching the gospel and was awaiting execution, all of which he seemed to take in stride. But when he mentions the names of people who had been his friends but had now either betrayed or abandoned him, he seems to take it quite personally:

> Demas has forsaken me, having loved this present world… Crescens [has departed] for Galatia, Titus for Dalmatia… Alexander the coppersmith did me much harm…At my first defense no one stood with me, but all forsook me (2 Timothy 4:10,14,16).

He's disappointed, but his letter also has a firm tone of acceptance:

> But the Lord stood with me and strengthened me, so that the message might be preached fully through me…And the Lord will deliver me from every evil work and preserve me for His heavenly kingdom (2 Timothy 4:17-18).

People had let him down, and Paul didn't pretend he was above feeling pain over their disappointing behavior. But at a deeper level, he could still accept his situation without approving of the wrong that had brought it about, because he kept sight of broader issues: his eternal reward, God's ability to sustain him even in prison, and the privilege he'd had as an evangelist and teacher. "Life," he seems to be saying, "is not as

I want it to be, and people have severely disappointed me. But in light of what I've enjoyed in this life, and what I anticipate in the next, I can accept all of it."

Of course, you're not Paul, and there's no imminent execution involved here. But I hope you can see the same principle at work in your own life, which is the principle of acceptance.

I've seen this at work in a female friend of mine whose daughter is a lesbian activist. Complicating matters, my friend had raised her daughter in a Christian home, and after her daughter came out, my friend began sponsoring conferences and ministries to assist people wanting to abandon homosexual behavior. In other words, the two became full-time workers for opposing (and sometimes mutually hostile) sociopolitical groups.

Obviously, they had a lot to argue about, but they had more than their differences to consider. They had history—years of love and family life, hard times they'd weathered together, common interests they still shared. So they decided, wisely, to just enjoy each other in spite of their differences. Realizing life is short, they decided not to waste it debating the same old pro-gay/anti-gay arguments. Instead, they called a truce and learned to enjoy the times they had together by concentrating on what they still had in common. In doing so, this Christian mother learned to *accept*, even when she couldn't possibly *approve*.

Are you ready to do the same? The apostle Paul shows us both the secret to and the benefit of reaching a point of acceptance. He said, in spite of all his hardships,

> Nevertheless I am not ashamed, for I know whom I have
> believed and am persuaded that He is able to keep what I
> have committed to Him until that Day (2 Timothy 1:12).

So what happens when homosexuality hits home? First, you cry. Then you argue with your loved one, perhaps even shout a bit. You question;

you agonize; you rage. You try to understand the person you love, perhaps never reaching a point of full understanding but trying all the same. You negotiate, renegotiate, and finally come to some sort of terms by which the two of you can still have a relationship.

Then you draw close to God—hopefully, closer than ever. In doing so, you strengthen your relationship with Him and others as well. You lean on friends, listen to mentors, rest a bit, and try to find a way to relax and even have a bit of fun.

You still grieve, and you still wait, but finally, you also accept. You're able to accept because, being closer to God than ever, your faith and patience have been strengthened. So you learn to enjoy your homosexual loved one without ever approving of homosexuality, and in doing so, your confidence grows to the point where you, having committed this beloved person to God, can say with more confidence than ever, "I know who I have believed, and am persuaded that He is able to keep that which I have committed—the person I love and who God loves even more—unto Him."

My hope is that, by the time you finish this book, this place of acceptance will be your place as well. May it be, and may it be soon.

Suggestions Before Moving On to Chapter 2

1. Determine which of the five stages of grief—denial, anger, bargaining, depression, acceptance—best describes what you're going through at this point.

2. Based on which stage you're in, determine what specific action you need to take to help yourself get through this part of the process. (See the "If this is where you are" section following whichever stage you see yourself in at this point.)

3. Determine under what terms you and your homosexual loved one can remain in a relationship. Are all these terms nonnegotiable, or can any of them be negotiated?

4. Plan specifically and clearly what you're going to do to protect your spiritual, emotional, and physical well-being during this difficult time.

5. What is your relationship with God like at this point? Close? Distant? Growing? Determine what you can do to draw closer to God and what steps you'll take to do so.

Chapter 2

"How Can This Be?"

Lives already broken by sin—anyone's sin—
fracture along lines we often cannot perceive.

—Mona Riley and Brad Sargent
Unwanted Harvest?

When we're appalled at the actions of someone we care about, we search for reasons for that behavior. So once we accept the fact that our loved one *is* homosexual, *why* he or she is homosexual often becomes the next issue.

It's a question that certainly plagued my father. When I first told him I'd been involved with men, after his initial explosion he settled into a sort of ongoing befuddlement. Time and again I'd catch him studying me, shaking his head, wondering.

"You were always masculine, Joe," he'd say, squinting at me like I was a science experiment. "You played football in school, you were in the jocks' fraternity, and Lord knows you've had your share of girlfriends. Now you say you've been having sex with men. How? How can this be?"

I never answered. How, after all, could I explain what I myself didn't understand? And therein lies the tension we experience when homosexuality hits home: Everyone—even the homosexual person—wants to know *why*, but no one seems to have the answer.

Does it even matter *why* the person you love is gay?

Well, yes, to a point it does matter, because whatever you think causes homosexuality will affect the way you respond to your loved one. If for example you think he chose to be gay, then you'll respond to him as you would toward anyone who has made the wrong choice—you'll expect him to simply choose *not* to be attracted to the same sex, and the problem will be solved. Or if you believe homosexuality is demonic in origin, you'll view your loved one as either possessed or, at the least, under the strong influence of dark forces. So whatever you think caused your loved one's homosexuality will have an impact on your relationship.

When we love a homosexual family member, we want to know *why*: Why does he feel this way? What caused it? And did I have anything—or nothing—to do with it?

For that reason, I'd like you to consider some of the prevailing theories on the causes of homosexuality. It won't change your position on the *ethics* of it—after all, if something is wrong, it's wrong, no matter what caused it—but it may give you a better understanding of the person you love, some of the factors that brought him to this point, and some of what he experienced long before he revealed his homosexuality to you. And at a time like this, that sort of understanding can only help.

But let's remember that our understanding is and always will be incomplete. We can learn more about homosexuality, and we should. But the more I learn about it, the more I realize we'll never *fully* understand this part of human sexuality, just as we'll never fully understand human sexuality itself. So as we approach the *why* question, a bit of humility is certainly in order. Let me suggest a five-point policy when trying to understand the *why's*:

1. Where the Bible is adamant, be adamant.

2. Where the Bible is silent, be open-minded.

3. When a theory *contradicts* what Scripture clearly teaches, *reject* it.

4. When a theory is *affirmed* by what Scripture teaches, *accept* it.

5. When a theory is neither confirmed nor denied by Scripture, *consider* it.

This is a policy I adopted long ago when studying psychology. Much of what my professors were teaching was, I knew, blatantly unbiblical. So when listening to lectures on humanist theories, I'd make a mental note to memorize the material so I could pass the test, then reject it in practice. That was a no-brainer.

At other times, I'd study writings on human development and child-raising that clearly had their roots in Judeo–Christian thought, so of course I embraced them as useful and true. And when a theory was presented that neither contradicted the Bible nor was affirmed by it, I'd note it with a question mark. Perhaps it was true; perhaps not. I would at least consider it.

That's the approach we'll take when reviewing theories on the cause of homosexuality.

What We *Do* Know

We can say five things with biblically based confidence concerning homosexuality, all of which have to do with the human condition in general or with homosexuality in particular.

1. We are *created beings,* created with a specific *intent* (see Genesis 1:26–2:23). One of the basics of the Christian faith is the concept of created intent, which teaches that we are created by a Maker who had a specific *intention* for our life experiences in general and our sexual experiences in particular. This belief is a cornerstone for our position on homosexuality because it sets the standard by which we decide what is or is not moral.

By this standard, questions of right versus wrong, or normal versus abnormal, are determined by whether or not a thing is in harmony with the intentions of our Maker. Our primary responsibility in life, then, is not to discover what feels natural to us or what seems right to us. That's secondary. What's primary is to discover and then align ourselves with the intentions of our Creator.

2. The created intent for the expression of human sexuality is fulfilled within the covenant of a *monogamous* and *heterosexual* union (see Matthew 19:4-6). When Jesus was questioned about the legitimacy of divorce, He answered plainly: God's original, created intention was that marriage be independent ("'A man shall leave father and mother and be joined to his wife'"), monogamous ("What God has joined together, let not man separate"), and heterosexual ("He…'made them male and female'"). We can conclude, then, that anything short of or apart from this is outside the boundaries of God's intentions.

3. We are a *fallen race*, and the Fall has marred every part of our experience, including our sexual experience (see Psalm 51:5; Romans 5:12-19). Paul's teaching in Romans 5, combined with David's remarks about his inherited sinfulness, is crucial to our understanding of homosexuality, even though the subject isn't mentioned in these scriptures. They explain why some things that are sinful may feel perfectly natural and good to us; while things that are right in God's sight may feel, to us, unnatural and difficult. We are a fallen race, beset with any number of sinful tendencies. Further, the Fall expresses itself differently through different people. We share a common curse in that each of us is born with a sin nature. But how that nature expresses itself is unique to the individual, leaving some people with a strong tendency toward violence, some with a weakness for lying, and still others with unnatural sexual tendencies.

4. Homosexual behavior is both a *manifestation* of fallen nature and a *violation* of created intent (see Leviticus 18:22;

20:13; Romans 1:26-27; 1 Corinthians 6:9-10; 1 Timothy 1:9-10). Many sexual behaviors are mentioned and condemned in both Testaments: adultery, incest, fornication, prostitution, and homosexuality are the most prominent. In light of the clear standard Christ set for human sexuality, these behaviors logically fall short of created design and are listed as moral violations in the Levitical law and in Paul's writings to the Corinthians and Timothy. Likewise, homosexuality is described in Paul's letter to the Romans as being unnatural and symptomatic of the larger problem of man's rebellion.

5. Homosexuals, like all people, are *redeemable*. As such, they can and often do repent and change (see 1 Corinthians 6:11). In his letter to the church in Corinth, Paul described some of the Corinthians as formerly being involved in homosexuality but having repented and become sanctified believers. This is good news indeed, both to you and your gay loved one, no matter what his or her current beliefs about homosexuality may be. There have always been, and always will be, those who reach a point at which they hunger for something more than what they've settled for in homosexual relationships. And when they reach that point, they become the very ones Paul refers to here: those who were (past tense) actively homosexual, but are now identified by their relation to Christ and their ongoing purity.

These five points constitute what we *do* know about homosexuality. We can be adamant about these positions and test all other theories in light of them.

Four Common Theories

You'll notice, though, that the five points above don't fully explain specifically why some people are attracted to the same sex. For a better understanding of that, let's now look at four of the most common theories on the cause and development of homosexuality.

The Inborn Theory

By now, your loved one may have concluded he or she was born gay and hopes you'll agree. After all, it's a simple answer to the complicated question of why, and it certainly relieves everyone involved of any sense of responsibility or guilt. That, combined with the fact that most homosexual people know from fairly early in life the way they feel, makes the born-gay theory both believable and convenient.

Yet the idea that people are born gay is relatively new. Historically, homosexuality in Western culture has been viewed as either intrinsically evil, a form of madness or, in more recent times, evidence of stunted psychosexual development.* And while no one theory on the cause of homosexuality has ever been universally accepted, the idea of a gay gene was not widely entertained until recently, not even by the homosexual population itself.

That changed in 1991, when two studies promoting the idea that homosexuality is inborn drew extravagant media attention, thereby incorporating the born-gay assumption once and for all into the public's consciousness.

First, Dr. Simon LeVay, a neuroscientist at the Salk Institute in La Jolla, California, reported a region of the brain called the INAH3 to be larger in heterosexual men than in homosexuals. He also found it to be larger in heterosexual men than in the women he studied. For that reason, he hypothesized that homosexuality might be inborn, and his findings were published in *Science* in August 1991.

Another study from the same year was hailed as proof of homosexuality's inborn nature. Psychologist J. Michael Bailey (a gay-rights advocate) of Northwestern University and psychiatrist Richard Pillard of Boston University School of Medicine (who is openly homosexual) compared sets of identical male twins to fraternal twins (whose genetic ties are less

---

* For a fuller treatment of the history of the Western view of homosexuality, see Ronald Bayer's *Homosexuality and American Psychiatry: The Politics of Diagnosis* (New York: Basic Books, 1981).

close). In each of the compared sets, at least one twin was homosexual.

Extensive media coverage made these studies common knowledge and led much of the public to believe a gay gene had been discovered. Many subsequent studies have been offered, none conclusive, yet all have been widely reported and assumed to be more "proof." Accordingly, the conventional wisdom on gays has become "They're born that way, God made them that way, so it must be normal."

Over the years that's become the common assumption: Homosexuality is inborn; therefore God made it; therefore it's good. Celebrities, educators, and cultural icons from Dear Abby to Oprah have gone on record saying as much, and a high percentage of the public has believed them.

That being the case, could genes or other inborn factors have anything to do with your loved one's homosexuality?

Possibly. Genes, after all, have much to do with our taste, preference, talents, and general capacities. Psychologist Warren Throckmorton, for example, has collected data from the American Psychological Association on behaviors influenced by genes and the percentages of people exhibiting these behaviors for strictly genetic reasons:

Attitudes about reading books	55%
Feelings about roller coasters	50%
Attitudes toward equality	55%[1]

In some cases, then, fairly normal behavior can be inspired by a person's genes. But the same can be said of behaviors we all agree are undesirable. Studies over the past 15 years indicate a variety of such behaviors may have their roots in genetics or biology. In 1983, the former director of the National Council on Alcoholism reported on a number of chemical events that can produce alcoholism; in 1991, the City of Hope Medical Center found a certain gene present in 77 percent of their alcoholic patients. Obesity and violent behavior are now thought to be genetically influenced; and even infidelity, according to research reported in *Time* magazine, may be in our genes!

Surely we're not going to say that obesity, violence, alcoholism, and adultery are legitimate because they were inherited. Likewise, we wouldn't say that people are doomed to become alcoholics or overeaters just because they are genetically vulnerable to these behaviors. Free will, choice, and discipline still have a great deal to do with how much these tendencies will affect a person's future.

So it is with homosexuality. Even if someday a so-called gay gene were to be discovered, it would not mean the person carrying that gene has no choice but to engage in same-sex relationships. Whether inborn or acquired, homosexual behavior is still, like all sexual contact apart from marriage, immoral. And immoral behavior cannot be legitimized by a quick baptism in the gene pool. It does not have to be indulged.

Remember that we are a fallen race, born in sin. Scripture teaches that we inherited a corrupt sin nature affecting us physically and spiritually:

> Behold, I was brought forth in iniquity; and in sin my mother conceived me (Psalm 51:5).

> Just as through one man sin entered the world, and death through sin…thus death spread to all men, because all sinned (Romans 5:12).

We were born spiritually dead (see John 3:5-6) and physically imperfect (see 1 Corinthians 15:1-54). Therefore we cannot assume that because something is inborn, it is also God-ordained. There are mental, psychological, physical, and sexual aspects of our beings that God never intended us to have. "Inborn," in short, cannot mean "divinely sanctioned."

The Developmental / Family Theory

One of the oldest, most hotly disputed beliefs about homosexuality is that it stems from problems arising between parent and child. Freud held to this belief, and mental health practitioners from his time onward assumed it to be true until the mid to late 1970s.

Building on Freudian thought, psychoanalyst Irving Bieber released a study of homosexual men in 1960 in which he concluded male homosexuality was, in most cases, evidence of a poor father–son relationship. His theory of the "family constellation"—a rejecting or passive father, a dominant mother, and a passive son—enjoyed broad acceptance for decades.

While this theory is dismissed vehemently by many pro-gay spokespersons, the number of public gay figures who report having this very sort of childhood lends it credibility.

Rosie O'Donnell, for example, has publicly described her early family life as "unsafe" and "very unhealthy." Olympic diving champion Greg Louganis writes in his autobiography that his stepfather routinely intimidated and abused him. Lesbian rock star Melissa Etheridge recalls her childhood environment as deeply wounding, leaving her with longings for a mother figure, which she tried to satisfy in lesbian relationships. Dr. Simon LeVay (mentioned earlier with regard to the born-gay theory) has admitted that his own upbringing—especially his relationship with his father—mirrored the classic Freudian theories on homosexuality. And Larry Kramer, the virulent gay activist and founder of the AIDS Coalition to Unleash Power (ACT UP), has written in detail about his ongoing battles with his dad during his formative years.

In fairness, other publicly gay figures report healthy, loving relations with their parents. Ellen DeGeneres, for example, cites her mother as unconditionally affectionate and caring, and Mrs. DeGeneres often stands with her daughter in public gay-related events. Religious activist Mel White has also challenged the family theory by pointing to his own strong ties to both his parents. Clearly, not all homosexual people had difficulties with their fathers or mothers. But many did—too many in fact for us to dismiss the family theory altogether.

In his book *Male Homosexuality* for example,* Dr. Richard Friedman cites 13 independent studies from 1959 to 1981 on the early family lives of homosexuals. Out of these 13, all but one concluded that, in the parent–child interactions of adult homosexuals, the subject's relationship with the parent of the same sex was unsatisfactory, ranging from distant and nonintimate to outright hostile. Most of the findings also indicated problems between the subjects and their parents of the opposite sex, but those problems were secondary in most cases.

An early perception, then, of rejection or indifference from the parent of the same sex can be seen in the backgrounds of many homosexually oriented adults.

As early as 1941, W.D. Fairbairn presented similar ideas when he stated,

> Frustration of his desire to be loved and to have his love accepted is the greatest trauma that a child can experience. Where relationships with outer objects (i.e. parents) are unsatisfactory, we also encounter such phenomena as… homosexuality and [these] phenomena should be regarded as attempts to salvage natural emotional relationships which have broken down.[2]

Does this mean that a faulty relationship with parents always creates homosexuality? Clearly not. Many heterosexuals grew up in families that were highly dysfunctional. Many boys have been raised by unloving and even cruel fathers whose mistreatment didn't cause their sons to turn to other men for sex. Many girls were brought up by uncaring mothers, yet these girls developed a normal sexual orientation. And yet these problems exist in the family backgrounds of many homosexually inclined adults.

So it may be possible, in my opinion, that your loved one's homosexuality had much to do with his or her relationship with the parent of

---

* New Haven, CT: Yale University Press, 1988.

the same sex. And if the loved one you're concerned about is your son or daughter, that parent may be you. But let's not be too quick to conclude that you are then to blame for the problem. It's not that simple.

First, let's remember that it's not what *actually happens* between parent and child that creates later problems. Instead, it's the way the child *perceives* his relationship to his parents to be, and the way he emotionally *responds* to that perception. (This may explain why one child's sexual development takes a different turn from that of a sibling's.)

Perception and *response* are the two key words here. In all relationships, we perceive the other party as having a certain attitude toward us, and we respond to the other party according to our own perception of that attitude. If we think somebody likes us, whether that person really does or not, we'll feel comfortable in the relationship and probably want the friendship. If we perceive someone else as being unfriendly and rejecting, we'll tend to avoid that person.

Likewise, a child may have had parents who loved and highly valued him, but for some reason the communication of that love got blurred. He may have perceived his father to be indifferent when in fact the father cared very much. Still, the child doesn't respond emotionally to what really is—only to what he *thinks* is real.

In both cases, whether the child experienced *actual* rejection from the parent of the same sex or simply *perceived* that rejection, he will have responded emotionally. And that emotional response is in many cases the beginning of strong, unfulfilled needs contributing to homosexual attractions.

This, according to the developmental theory, is how it often begins: A normal yet unmet need for bonding with a member of the same sex remains unsatisfied, leaving the boy or girl yearning for, then seeking out, fulfillment of these normal needs through abnormal behaviors such as homosexuality. (For a more complete treatment of the origins of homosexuality, please see my book *Desires in Conflict,* Harvest House, 2003.)

Let me reiterate that no one theory on the development of sexual orientation fits all cases. And indeed, when we look at the developmental theory, it relies largely on the recollections of the individual, recollections which may or may not be accurate. So I by no means advocate applying this theory to your own situation. I simply recognize that it seems, in my experience, to have validity in many cases.

The Violation Theory

The Bible records a harrowing episode in King David's family history when his daughter Tamar was violated by her stepbrother Amnon. In 2 Samuel 13, we see Amnon, obsessed with lust over Tamar, plotting her rape with his cousin. Feigning illness, he asked her to bring food to his bedchamber, and when she complied, he attacked her. Knowing her status as a virgin would be lost in the most dishonoring way, leaving her unacceptable for any future husband, she begged Amnon to release her. But he persisted, using and then discarding her brutally.

She spent the rest of her days, according to Scripture, "a desolate woman."

Sexual violation is a peculiar evil that has left many a boy or girl desolate. The effects of it can be guessed at but never really measured. Among all crimes, it is one of the most sinister and devastating. And often, the devastation shows itself in sexual confusion.

Molestation, like parent–child conflicts, is often cited by gays and lesbians as part of their history. Rosie O'Donnell reports being molested as a girl. Greg Louganis recounts his earliest sexual experience as occurring with a stranger who seduced him as a teenager. Rev. Troy Perry, founder of the largest gay denomination today, was raped by his stepfather's friend, and Melissa Etheridge was repeatedly molested by her older sister. While all of the above-named people consider homosexuality normal and no doubt would deny the role these violations played in their current sexual preferences, we can't ignore the impact they must have had.

And yet, as with the parenting theory, the cause-and-effect correlation of early abuse and later homosexuality is not conclusive. Many abuse survivors are heterosexual; many homosexuals were not abused. But homosexuality follows sexual abuse often enough for us to consider it as a contributor in many cases. I've seen the connection in too many of my own clients to dismiss it. Most of the women I've worked with who were involved in lesbianism have also endured sexual abuse; usually but not always at the hands of a family member. My male clients as well report a high rate of abuse in their backgrounds (well over 50 percent), indicating its effect on their adult sexuality.

How, then, can sexual violation contribute to homosexuality? Generally, two different things could come into play, depending on the victim's gender. A violated girl will often conclude men are unsafe and destructive, closing off future potential bonding with a male partner. Barbara Swallow, a former lesbian and author who directs a ministry called Free Indeed, recalls how her uncle's violation of her as a girl left her feeling it was "unsafe" to be female. The male role seemed safer; males themselves seemed lethal. I've found her story to be typical of many of the women I've worked with.

But a violated boy may, ironically, find the experience binds him to other males as sexual partners rather than as friends or comrades. Several of my male clients confessed that, as confusing and frightening as the molestations were, their experiences did seem to heighten their sexual appetites and set the stage for further homosexual encounters.*

This theory opens the possibility that someone you love was violated. But you should by no means assume the possibility is a fact unless you have objective proof or your loved one's firsthand testimony. So please don't jump to the conclusion after reading this chapter that he or she is an abuse survivor. Remember, no one theory fits all cases. If your family

---

* *The Wounded Heart* by Dan Allender (NavPress, 1990) gives a full and excellent overview of the effects of sexual abuse.

member has not indicated such a thing and you have no evidence it ever happened, then assume there are other reasons for the homosexuality.

And while we're on the subject, please disregard the "repressed memory" notion. The evidence is overwhelming on the matter—when people are traumatized, they vividly remember the trauma in practically all cases. So there's no reason to assume your loved one may not remember, or is repressing, some early violation. That sort of repression is rare and seldom verifiable.

The bottom line? In many cases, early sexual violation plays a role in adult homosexuality. And although it should never be taken for granted that an adult homosexual was molested, it can be and often is the case.

So if in your family discussions you learn your gay loved one was violated, refer him or her to a licensed Christian mental-health provider immediately. No matter where your loved one stands on homosexuality—whether embracing or rejecting it—he or she needs to deal with the emotional aftereffects of the abuse. Do all within your power to encourage this.

The Demon / Unclean Spirit Theory

Although most Christians do not consider homosexuality to be a form of demon possession, I'll mention this theory because there's still considerable confusion about what role, if any, demons play in the matter. Among believers from charismatic or Pentecostal background especially, the possibility of spiritual forces creating or sustaining homosexuality is often considered. And while there is not a body of literature supporting or explaining this approach, I hear from enough parents and family members to know that when homosexuality hits home, a demon may be seen as the culprit.

This conclusion is often drawn from the Gospel accounts of Jesus's driving out unclean spirits. Since homosexuality is viewed by many Christians as a form of uncleanness, some assume the uncleanness is a spirit oppressing or even possessing the homosexual. And in response, varying forms of exorcism or deliverance have been recommended.

Gay activist Mel White mentions such rituals as a part of his past attempts to overcome homosexuality. Similarly, gay speaker Mike Williams, who used to testify to having overcome homosexuality but has since recanted and now testifies to being both gay and Christian, recalls how a well-known charismatic leader attempted to drive homosexual "spirits" from him. The results, predictably, were (and are) tragic.

And yet we often try to demonize what we cannot understand. So while heterosexuals can relate to the problem of lusting for the opposite sex, most are baffled or repulsed at the very thought of lusting for the same sex. That leads many to draw the erroneous conclusion that what is *unnatural* must be *demonic*.

That's a conclusion the Bible doesn't support. In both Leviticus 18 and 20, homosexuality is mentioned among many other sins, mostly sexual, and most having nothing to do with the occult. Likewise, when Paul mentioned homosexuals to the Corinthians, he categorized them as but one of many types of sinners, all of whom are dealing with sins of the flesh, not demons to be cast out.

Even more significant is Jesus's own take on such sins when He indicates the root of the problem in Mark's Gospel:

> From within, out of the heart of men, proceed evil thoughts, adulteries, fornications, murders...All these evil things come from within and defile a man (Mark 7:21-23).

Throughout the New Testament, whenever sexual sin is mentioned, it is cited as a problem of the flesh to be dealt with through repentance and discipline. When, for example, Paul rebuked the Corinthian church for allowing a member to engage in relations with his stepmother, he called for church discipline, not a deliverance ritual (see 1 Corinthians 5).

That's not to say we're not engaged in spiritual warfare. We are indeed fighting an intense spiritual battle whenever we bring our gay loved one before God's throne in prayer, interceding and pleading. But the sin itself—whether natural or unnatural—remains a problem of the flesh and the soul, rather than a problem that is inherently demonic.

The bottom line? Your family member is in sin. One that's hard to relate to, perhaps, but a sin nonetheless. And to be in sin is a far cry from being possessed or in bondage to an evil spirit, so your loved one is almost certainly neither possessed nor oppressed.

That doesn't rule out the strong possibility—even the likelihood—of deception, which we know to be the devil's forte. After all, Paul referred to nonbelievers as those whose minds were blinded by Satan:

> Even if our gospel is veiled, it is veiled to those who are perishing, whose minds the god of this age has blinded, who do not believe, lest the light of the gospel of the glory of Christ, who is the image of God, should shine on them (2 Corinthians 4:3-4).

Satan's strategy in leading humans astray, whether the arena is doctrinal or moral, is to deceive an individual into thinking that what God has forbidden is not really wrong or destructive but rather is life-enhancing. So it was in the garden when Satan tempted Eve; so it may well be with your loved one. The sin of homosexuality is human in nature, but the belief that sin is not really sin comes not from human nature alone but from an ancient and evil messenger.

So how can this be? How did this person we love develop feelings and passions that we would have never wished for him and that, in all likelihood, he would have never wished for himself?

Genetically, he may have a personality that is more susceptible to some of the influences that can create homosexuality. That's inborn and is no one's fault. That doesn't mean he was born gay; rather, he may have been born with a personality more *vulnerable* to homosexuality than most people's. Then, probably within the first few years of life, he developed strong but unmet needs for bonding with the same sex, needs that were not, for whatever reason, satisfied. Or this person's normal development may have been interrupted by violation or abuse, causing an inevitable disruption in normal sexual responses.

The chances are slim to nonexistent that this person's homosexuality is caused by demonic forces, although forces like that exist and can be part of the problem in some cases.

And of course, there are probably other factors neither you nor your loved one will ever be able to identify. Remember, although we may know on biblical authority that something is unnatural and wrong, that doesn't mean we'll fully understand what causes it. So while the points I've mentioned above may apply to your family member, there might be other reasons for the homosexuality, reasons you'll never fully identify or understand.

But for now, there are things you can know for certain:

1. You and your loved one still have a relationship, however imperfect.

2. Your loved one is still the same person he or she was before you found out about the homosexuality. It's not as though you no longer know the person; you now actually know *more* about him or her. And what you know now doesn't undo everything you've known before. In short, everything you've loved about this person all along is still there, intact and waiting to be enjoyed.

3. God is relentlessly at work in the person you love. You may not be the one who'll change his or her mind about homosexuality; you may have little or no influence at this point. But God has thousands of means at His disposal for continuing to woo your loved one to Himself, and He is still employing them.

That you *can* know. And in that, you can rest.

Points to Consider from Chapter 2

1. When trying to understand a human problem, it's best to be adamant only when and where the Bible is adamant. And since the Bible does not clearly state why people become homosexual—although it clearly condemns homosexual behavior—we cannot be sure in every case what causes people to become attracted to the same sex.

2. We can accept that something is wrong even if we don't fully understand what caused it. For example, we do not know what causes some people to be more violent or aggressive than others, but we hold a clear moral position on violence. So it is with homosexuality—not knowing in all cases what created it does not nullify our ability to object to it on moral grounds.

3. The most commonly held theories on the causes of homosexuality are the genetic (or inborn) theory, the developmental (or family) theory, the disruption/violation theory, and the demonic/unclean spirit theory. Each has its weaknesses and each could have merit. But no one theory should be assumed to apply to all people.

Chapter 3

Loving a Gay Son or Daughter

When we have children,
we release hostages to fate.

—John F. Kennedy

f there were warning signs, the father didn't see them. And if he had
seen them, he probably wouldn't have guessed what they meant. So
by the time he knew there was a problem, much less how serious it was,
he was clueless as to what had gone wrong. He only knew his son had
made a decision—a wrong decision, one he was liable to spend his life
regretting. But the young man was determined, leaving his father to
feel that agonizing combination of yearning and helplessness that is, for
parents especially, the high price of love.

There's much we don't know about the events leading up to the
prodigal son's decision to leave home, since Jesus related only the barest
details of the story. It appears in the fifteenth chapter of Luke's Gospel as
part of Jesus's response to the scribes and Pharisees when they objected
to His association with "sinners," and is used both to rebuke their
self-righteousness and to illustrate the patient and loving heart of God.

Lessons from the Prodigal's Story

Emphasis is usually placed on the father's acceptance of the son at the end of the story. But let's consider the father's *pain*—much like God's, and much like yours, I'm sure—when he first discovered his son's rebellion, watched him leave, then waited for his return.

1. You Did Not Create or Commit Your Child's Sin

We can first assume that this father had done his job and done it well. He not only had two sons, but as the story progresses, we see he had servants, property, and other goods his sons would inherit. That meant hard work, planning, and the long hours of stress and watchfulness required of any man who wants to provide well for his family. In short, he had been a good dad. Yet his goodness didn't prevent his son's rebellion or the many problems he had been unaware of that led up to it. Therefore the prodigal's sin cannot be taken as an indictment of his father.

Does that mean this "good dad" was a "perfect dad"? Impossible. Since all have sinned and come short of the glory of God, we can conclude that all mothers and fathers have sinned and come short of perfect parenthood. Every year our children grow, we add more items—our unkind words, neglect, reactions, impatience, and an assortment of well-intentioned mistakes—to our list of regrets. And by the time the kids are grown, that list has become a report card with at least a few D's or F's, no matter how hard we tried for all A's.

No doubt, then, when his son left home, this man began an excavation to unearth his own failures. *What did I do wrong that caused him to make such a bad choice?* he must have asked himself. And of course he found hundreds of mistakes and sins of his own, perhaps concluding that his shortcomings as a father had created the problem.

He was only partially right. He *was* imperfect, since an imperfect man can't be anything but an imperfect parent. There were times he had lost his temper or had been too busy to pay attention to his son or spent too many hours working or had been too harsh in discipline, all of which spells *imperfect*. But whether or not his imperfections caused the problem was another question. And more important, even if his imperfections had contributed to his son's *attitude,* did that make him responsible for his son's *decision?*

Clearly not. But try telling that to a parent in pain! You, for example, are probably looking at your relationship with your son or daughter under a microscope. You're examining the early years, perhaps in light of theories you've read on homosexuality, and you're wondering: Did she get enough love? Were my spouse and I affectionate enough with her? Did she get enough time, attention, discipline, prayer, concern? Did I tell her often enough how much I loved her? Was I as a parent all I could have been?

And the answer of course is no. No child was raised as well as he could have been. The question, then, isn't whether or not you failed in any way. You did, as we all have and will. The question is whether or not your imperfections caused your son or daughter to become homosexual.

And again the answer is no, because homosexuality is not caused by one influence alone. As I tried to show earlier, there's a constellation of influences involved. Based on all available research, when we try to pinpoint what creates homosexuality, we find at least five factors:

1. the child's genes (whether or not he's born with a genetic susceptibility to gender-identity problems)

   combined with:

2. his relationship with his parents

   combined with:

3. his relationship with siblings and peers

   combined with:

4. possible violations or traumas

combined with:

5. other factors we're still unaware of

Perhaps some or all of these combined, not one alone, create the homosexual orientation.

Now let's take a worst-case view of your parenting. Suppose your relationship with your son or daughter fit the developmental theory mentioned in the previous chapter. Suppose that, as a father, you were emotionally distant from your son; or as a mother, you were too dominant or too involved in his life. Or if your daughter is lesbian, you as a mother were uninvolved; or as her father, you were overinvolved or somehow abusive. In that case, you may be part of the problem (notice factor 2 above)—but only *part*. Other factors beyond your control, such as 1, 3, 4, and 5, also may have come into play. So the worst you could say in such a case is that your relationship was faulty and may have *contributed to*, but not *created*, your son's or daughter's homosexuality. (Remember that many heterosexuals were raised by parents who fit the above patterns.)

Likewise, let's take a best-case viewpoint. Suppose, imperfect as you may be, your parenting was exemplary by any reasonable standard. You loved your child, and the balance of affection and discipline in your home was right about where it should have been. That alone can't prevent factors 1, 3, 4, and 5 from happening, can it? So your parenting may in fact have very little to do with the situation.

This is the hard lesson the prodigal's father had to grapple with: A parent's love cannot prevent destructive influences from affecting a daughter or son. And that, I'm sure, is what John F. Kennedy meant by "releasing hostages to fate."

I didn't know what fear was until I had children. As much as I love it, fatherhood introduced a whole new set of terrors to me. Only then did the possibility of my sons' having accidents, getting kidnapped, or being brutalized by peers become the stuff of my nightmares. I've had to realize I will always be torn between two hard facts: my longing to protect my children from harm or sin, and my inability to fully protect them from either.

What to do? If you can see where you're guilty of mistakes or wrongdoing as a parent, admit it and take responsibility for it. You may have apologies or explanations to make to your son or daughter, and now would be a good time to make them. But it's wrong to assume whatever mistakes you made *created* your son's or daughter's sexual preference. You may—or may not—have contributed to it. Your influence is limited; so limited that you could not, even if you had wanted to, have caused your loved one's homosexuality.

Do what the prodigal's father had to do at some point: Be realistic when you assign blame. Take responsibility for whatever wrong you may have done to your child, but refuse to accept responsibility for his sexual orientation and for what he has decided to do with it.

2. Your Influence Is Limited

Please note: This section is written primarily for parents with adult sons or daughters. If your child is underage, please balance this section with the following chapter: "When Your Teen Says 'I'm Gay.'"

One of the most pervasive myths we believe about love is that it endows us with near-supernatural power. This myth is especially potent when it comes to our children. When we love a child deeply, it's easy to assume the depth of our love will give us influence over that child.

After all, from Day One they rely on us for everything, from the basics to the luxuries; in fact, our natural instincts to provide for them start flowing when they're still in the womb. So long as our children are indeed children, the marriage of our protective urges and their vulnerability is a perfect fit.

But to every parent's dismay, no timer has been set on our instincts. They stay intact, sturdy and deep, long after our offspring reach adulthood. Worse still, while our protective feelings refuse to budge, *their* instincts toward independence come along just fine. This leaves millions of parents longing to exert much more influence over their grown sons or daughters than they are ever likely to have.

So a huge part of the difficulty you have with a prodigal lies in the adjusting of roles. Yours was initially that of primary caregiver and main influencer. When he was a child, you oversaw virtually every part of his life. Your opinion was crucial; your decisions pretty much dictated the details of his day. In short, you had both authority and influence.

Then, shortly before adolescence, you noticed a shift in clout. Now the opinion of peers seemed to carry much more weight than your own—a normal but difficult developmental phase. At that point, your *influence* faded even though your *authority* as a parent was still in force.

Finally, when he reached young adulthood, your role shifted yet again as you lost both influence and authority, going from provider-teacher to consultant. And of course people deal with consultants on *their* terms, not on the consultants', an uncomfortable but necessary truth all parents in this role have to deal with.

The prodigal's father certainly had to. His grown son had made a decision, and it seemed nonnegotiable. We do not know whether the father pleaded, threatened, or argued; we only know he eventually gave his son what he wanted: his inheritance and his freedom. No doubt he stated his position: "You're wrong; you don't know what's waiting out there for you; you're breaking my heart." But *stating* his position and *forcing* his position would have been two very different things indeed.

Dealing with that tension is especially hard when we have the perspective of age and experience our children can't possibly have. It's the curse of knowing how needlessly difficult they're making their lives but being powerless to force that knowledge into their heads. Had this son attempted to leave home when he was still a young boy, the father could have refused to hand over his inheritance, based on the son's age and status. But no more. Letting him go wasn't just the reasonable thing to do; it was the only thing to do.

When I was a toddler, I became fascinated with a steep road leading down to a bridge just outside my front yard. I had a little fire truck I loved to pedal around in, and that steep, very dangerous road sure looked fun to me. Dad, naturally, wouldn't have it. He'd walk beside me while I rode my pedal truck, keeping an eye on where I was heading, which meant thrill-seeking was out of the question.

One morning, though, while walking with me, he struck up a long conversation with a neighbor, so I seized the opportunity and charged down the hill. I didn't even notice Dad sprint toward me and catch up, but I did notice it when he flipped the pedal truck over before it started down the decline, toppling me out and ruining my fun. I was not happy, but he didn't care. He knew where I had been headed, so as any good father would have, he stopped me by any means.

But when I was in my twenties, pursuing an ungodly lifestyle, I was too big to topple. He could only watch me go down the hill, a much larger one this time, on a course he couldn't keep me from pursuing. He was a prodigal's father; he had no choice but to let go. And I truly believe letting go, then watching and waiting, was the most difficult challenge he ever had to face as a father.

Your influence is limited, even when you're right. The prodigal's father was a good dad who had provided for, loved, and exercised authority over his son for a season. But when the season ended, he said his piece, respected the free will God had given his son, and let go.

We can only imagine what his prayers were like that night. They cannot have been much different from your own.

3. God's Ability to Influence Our Loved One Is Still Intact

The Jamieson, Fausset, and Brown commentary on the story of the prodigal makes a point that's worth our attention. Speaking of the moment the father allowed the son his freedom, the commentators note,

> Thus God, when His service no longer appears a perfect freedom, and when man promises himself something far better elsewhere, allows man to make the trial. And he shall discover, if need be by saddest proof, that to depart from Him is not to put off the yoke, but only to exchange a light yoke for a heavy one, and one gracious Master for a thousand imperious tyrants and lords.

The father's voice no longer had influence, so he let go. But God's grip wasn't loosened. He began speaking clearly through circumstances and consequences after two other means of speaking had been ignored.

First, God had spoken through His Word. Let's assume, not illogically, that the father had raised his son on the Scriptures, so the prodigal grew up knowing the importance of loving God and honoring His ways. But at some point, probably early in life and very secretly, he entertained other voices as well.

Maybe he and his young friends exchanged stories they'd heard about harlots or drunken orgies or any number of heathen practices. Something darkly mysterious about it all might have appealed to him (not unlike what many teens experience when they first stumble onto ungodly materials via the Internet), causing him to tuck away the future possibility of seeing for himself what "it" was like.

The boy may have already been having inner conflicts his father knew nothing about. His older brother's attitude, which we see toward the end of the story, suggests tension between them—maybe a rivalry for the father's affection or some long-standing hostility never fully resolved. At any rate, what the boy knew of the Scriptures was at some point ignored. He was forming a decision to go his own way, right or wrong.

God then must have spoken to his conscience. He knew truth, though he knew little of the consequences ignoring the truth could bring. So by the time he made his announcement to his father, his heart was already, no doubt, hardened, having rejected the truths he'd been taught and being filled with anticipation of whatever the world held for him. Conscience, like Scripture, had by then been dismissed.

Eventually, circumstances and consequences became the voices he could no longer ignore. The money squandered; the harlots long gone once the funds went dry; the revelry over; hardship closing in—these would now speak, and at full volume. Long after the father's voice was muted, the Father's voice thundered.

God has spoken in His Word, which a person may ignore. God will then speak to the conscience, which may also be ignored. He will then speak through circumstances which a person cannot as easily ignore. All of which means God has hardly exhausted the resources through which He can speak to your prodigal.

Meanwhile, you and your child still have a relationship to preserve. So, to help you and your loved one set terms for the future of your relationship, let me offer some suggestions for *clarifying* three points.

1. Clarify your son's or daughter's position on homosexuality.
Ascertain where he or she stands on homosexuality by asking, Have you decided this is normal and moral, or are you still deciding? And on what basis will you make, or have you made, this decision?

When someone says, "I'm gay," that doesn't answer the question as to how the person feels about homosexuality and why. In other words, two questions are primary: Has the person truly decided he's attracted to the same sex, and is he what we'll call gay-affirming? *Gay-affirming* means "holding a belief that homosexuality is normal and legitimate." So "I'm gay" can mean any of the following:

1. *Decided and gay-affirming*: "I'm gay, that's fine with me, and I'm waiting for Mom and Dad to finally accept it."

2. *Undecided*: "I'm attracted to the same sex, but I'm not sure whether or not it's okay to act on these attractions. I'm still deciding, but I at least want to be honest about the existence of these attractions."

3. *Decided but not gay-affirming*: "These attractions are definitely here, but I know homosexuality is wrong, so I don't intend to act on them. I intend to resist them."

To get a better understanding of where your relationship with your son or daughter is headed, ask which of the above best describes him or her. After listening carefully, then you can act as follows:

1. *If he is decided but not gay-affirming*: That means he is in essence admitting that homosexuality is a *temptation*, but he's also rejecting it as a *way of life*. Offer your wholehearted support and appreciation for his honesty. Make sure he knows you're aware of how hard it is to say no to something the rest of the world seems to be saying is normal, and reassure him he has an ally and friend in you. If he's unaware of resources to help him keep his commitment to purity, refer him to the organizations and books listed in the back of this book.

2. *If she is undecided*: Ask candidly on what basis she will be making her decision. Scripture? Her feelings? Professional or academic opinion? Don't ask with the goal of challenging her answer— make it clear you only want to better understand how she will come to one of the most momentous decisions she'll ever make.

   Ask if she's open to talking to a Christian counselor or pastor whose viewpoint may be more traditional and who can offer a different perspective than the one she's probably been hearing. If she consents, refer to the resources listed in the back of this book.

But if she prefers not to, I strongly suggest you not push it. I've seen too many parents pressure their grown sons or daughters into counseling, with predictably bad results. I can almost guarantee you, if you push her or him into a counselor's office, you will not only *not* get the desired results, but your son or daughter will resent you deeply for the intrusion.

3. *If he is decided and gay-affirming*: Ask what, if anything, he's expecting of you. Agreement? Discussion? Conversion to his way of thinking? Again, the goal here is not to start an argument but rather to get a better idea of his expectations. This will help you clarify your own position and negotiate the relationship from here on.

2. Clarify your own position on homosexuality. Don't beat a dead horse by repeating, every time you see your son or daughter, what the Bible says and why you disapprove of homosexuality. That's unnecessary. But make certain you've clarified, once and for all, where you stand. I find it helpful to use the five points mentioned in chapter 2 when articulating reasons for objecting to homosexuality. Yet they don't include all that needs to be said at this point. Let me also suggest you make sure your son or daughter knows the following:

- You know he or she didn't ask for these feelings.

- You appreciate his or her honesty.

- Your position on the matter is still unchangeable.

- You want to protect your relationship through mutual respect and, as much as possible, mutual understanding.

- You may never agree on this issue, but you're committed to not letting that disagreement ruin your relationship.

3. Clarify your fears. "I'm scared to death now that my son has told me he's gay," I've often heard. "I'm worried about AIDS, but I also fear for his future. I've read about high rates of alcoholism and abuse among gays and lesbians and that their relationships don't tend to last. So now that he's come out, what should I expect his life to be like?"

While there are several things to fear, there's no reason to believe all the things you fear for your son or daughter will inevitably happen.

True, the rate of HIV infection remains much higher among homosexual men in America than among heterosexuals. But not every man who is homosexual is sexually active; not every homosexual who is sexually active engages in the sexual practices that transmit the AIDS virus. So it would be a grave mistake to assume your son is in immediate danger just because of his recent disclosure. What brings risk into his life is not his homosexual orientation, but how he chooses to conduct himself sexually.

Likewise, no matter what you've heard about the gay lifestyle, remember, there is a good deal of variety in the lifestyles of homosexual men and women. Many gays are very promiscuous; many aren't. Some settle into long-term relationships; some have short-lived affairs; still others prefer lifelong celibacy.

For that matter, there really is no such thing as a typical homosexual person. Although most seem to be politically liberal, many are conservative. Some are flamboyant and easily recognized; many are entirely undistinguishable. So at this point, please do *not* assume your daughter or son is going to live a certain way just because you've heard of the way some or even many homosexuals live.

Instead of assuming, *ask*. Ask how he or she lives. Tell your loved one plainly what your fears are and ask if he or she can help you by answering your questions honestly. That will give you a more accurate portrait of what you can expect, which can only help to ease family tensions and misunderstanding. I've known cases in which this approach has been more than helpful.

One mother, for example, came to me for a consultation. She was living with a twofold dread. First, she dreaded the problems she thought her son would have as a young gay man, problems she had both read and heard about. After he came out to her, she had picked up several books on male homosexuality, most of them written from a Christian perspective. While there was much valuable information in these books, they had also frightened her by offering statistics on the prevalence of promiscuity among gay men and the chances that disease, alcoholism, suicide, violence, and drug use could plague her son as well. No wonder she lived in fear! Thoughts of her son's engaging in dangerous, bizarre activities became a source of daily torment.

But she was just as tormented by the fear of losing him. They'd already argued about homosexuality, and their positions were clear: He was gay, she disapproved; but she had agreed not to badger him. Afterward she started hearing the stories and reading the materials about gay men, which terrified her. But since she'd promised to drop the subject, she stifled the urge to talk to him about his lifestyle and, more specifically, her concerns. She was trapped between her promise to respect his choices and her need to better understand what those choices were.

I suggested it was possible to ask these questions without "preaching." She wasn't, after all, trying to change him as much as she was trying to understand. So in an honest and tearful conversation, she told him, "I know you've decided you're gay, and I'm not trying to change you. But I've read that so many gay men have hundreds of partners, and that they're in danger of AIDS and other diseases as well as drug use. Can you at least tell me if that's true? Do you use drugs? Do you have several partners? Honey, please just help me understand how you live, because I'm so worried!"

Far from being offended, her son was moved by her concerns and was happy to relieve them. He was not promiscuous, never used drugs, drank occasionally, and knew all the do's and don'ts about unprotected sex.

This wasn't entirely satisfying to her. She wasn't convinced there was such a thing as safe sex, and she brought up realistic concerns about condom effectiveness and breakage. And knowing that her son lived a responsible life in many ways couldn't negate her objections to his homosexuality. Still, it was a huge relief to learn he did not fit the profile of a reckless, hedonistic young man flirting with death.

So clarify your fears. Doing so can only enhance communication and trust between you and your child.

These three clarifications will help you know what to expect of your son or daughter at this point. They also will give you an idea of what sorts of things you'll need to negotiate, which we'll discuss in chapter 7.

But before moving on, as the parent of a prodigal, will you take a moment to review Jeremiah's words—God's words, really—to parents in pain?

> Refrain your voice from weeping, and your eyes from tears; for your work shall be rewarded, says the LORD, and they [your children] shall come back from the land of the enemy. There is hope in your future, says the LORD, that your children shall come back to their own border (Jeremiah 31:16-17).

You can't miss the threefold message here:

God *sees.* He sees both your beloved daughter or son, and He sees your tears.

God *perseveres.* He continues His efforts long after human effort has exhausted itself.

God holds out *hope,* for both you and your children.

So in confidence of His ongoing work in your adult gay loved ones, you can now begin negotiating the boundaries of your relationship. That topic will be addressed in chapter 7.

Ten Other Issues
Parents Frequently Ask About

1. "I've been told the suicide rate among gay teenagers is high and that the primary reason is that parents reject them because of their homosexuality. I don't reject my son, but could my refusal to say, 'Gay is okay' actually damage him and put him at risk for suicide or other problems?"

   This concern is based largely on a faulty report submitted to the Secretary of Health and Human Services in 1989. The gist of the report was that suicide among gay teenagers accounted for a third of all teen suicides. Although the report was roundly discredited for its flaws in methodology and conclusion, the myth was born and has been repeated so often it has come to be accepted as conventional wisdom.

   Your belief that homosexuality is wrong will not damage your son, nor will your insistence that he live within the boundaries you set in your home.

   Of course, if you call him names, humiliate him, tell him his homosexuality makes him worse than other people, disown him, wish death or injury upon him, or otherwise abuse him physically or psychologically, then yes—you will definitely be damaging him. But to hold a belief about sex and promote that belief with your minor children is neither a form of rejection nor abuse. Rather, it's a quaint thing called *parenting*.

2. "My daughter has told me she doesn't want my husband to know about her lesbianism at this point. She has asked me to keep it to myself, but is that the right thing to do?"

No, it isn't. Your daughter is asking you to keep secrets from your husband, which is a surefire way of putting a wedge between the two of you. Explain to her that her request is unfair and you don't intend to comply. But do give her the option of telling him herself. Let her know that, if she wishes, you'll refrain briefly—a day or so—from talking to your husband about this. During that time, she can tell him herself. But if, after a couple of days, she still hasn't told him, then you should. He's entitled to know and, more important, it's wrong for your daughter to ask you to close a door of communication with your spouse.

3. "My son was raised Christian, and he claims that, even though he's gay, he's still a believer. I don't want to cut him off, but when I read in 1 Corinthians 5:11 that we should not have anything to do with a Christian who's living in open sin, does that apply to family members as well?"

In 1 Corinthians 5:11 Paul says, "I have written to you not to keep company with anyone named a brother, who is sexually immoral, or covetous, or an idolater, or a reviler, or a drunkard, or an extortioner—not even to eat with such a person."

I'm convinced this Scripture does *not* apply to family members. If it did, it would mean Christian husbands and wives would have to literally stop living together if one of them drank too much, raged, or showed evidence of idolatry. Likewise, it would mean Christian children would have to refuse to be in the same room with their Christian parents if those parents were involved in such sins. And obviously this would all contradict other Scriptures commanding us toward family harmony. So while I do believe we are commanded to withdraw from a believer (but not a blood relative) who is committing such sins, I do not believe these verses compel us to withdraw from our own family members.

4. "We're supporting our daughter through college, but she recently told us she's in a lesbian relationship. Since my husband and I disapprove of homosexuality, should we withdraw her tuition support? If we don't, aren't we encouraging her in this lifestyle?"

No, you're not. Putting her through college is a way of supporting her education and future career, not her lifestyle. Remember, the prodigal son's father did give him his inheritance (see Luke 15:12) even though he knew his son would most likely be living in sin. In doing so, he was supporting his *son*, not his son's *sin*.

If your daughter were asking you to financially back a cause or organization you don't believe in, that would be another matter. But withholding tuition will accomplish nothing and will only be seen as a form of punishment and manipulation. Helping her acquire a degree will improve her potential and future, no matter what she chooses to do with her sexuality.

5. "My son and his partner are adopting a child. And not long ago a friend told us, 'My daughter and her partner are having a child through artificial insemination.' What role, if any, should we as grandparents play in this?"

Your son is in sin; the child involved is not. (An out-of-wedlock pregnancy, for example, produces a child under the wrong circumstances, but the child itself could hardly be considered wrong and should be welcomed and cared for.)

That being the case, this child deserves all the love and support you can give. By all means be involved in the child's life to the fullest extent your son will allow and be a grandparent as you would be to any of your other children's children. Your son will need and appreciate any help you can offer, and there really is no moral compromise involved here. A new life is coming into your home. No matter the circumstances bringing it, it is—as is all life—sacred and precious.

6. "Our daughter is in her twenties and has come out to us. We have younger children still living with us at home, and they love their sister very much. Should we tell them about her, and if so, how should we tell them?"

At some point, yes, you'll need to tell them. So ask your daughter to let you be the one to do so, because you want to determine when and how this is disclosed.

Judge the timing for this as you would judge the timing for discussing any sensitive subject with your kids—determine their level of maturity and trust your instincts, much as you would with the "sex talk." (It's hard to say at what age kids in general are ready for that either, but your instincts are a pretty good guide.)

Then, when you feel they're ready, include the following points when you tell them about their sister:

- You love your daughter very much, you always will, and you hope they always will too.

- Their sister has decided she's a homosexual. You don't approve, and you're praying she'll change her mind about this, but for now this is what she's decided.

- You're not going to compromise your beliefs, and you won't ever allow anything to be practiced or expressed in the home that violates your moral principles.

- As much as possible, you want to keep the family together. You're not sure at this point how this will affect the family's future, but that will largely depend on what you and their sister can agree on when it comes to family visits and policies.

- You'll answer whatever questions they have as honestly as you can. If they need to talk with a counselor or pastor about this, you'll make an appointment for them.

- You want them to be honest with you about their feelings. If they're angry, confused, or upset, you want them to feel comfortable talking it over with you or with their sister, if she's open to that.

Then let your daughter know you've had this talk with her siblings. Emphasize that you hope her relationship with them will stay close, but make sure she understands the need to respect your teaching and boundaries in the home, especially regarding your younger kids.

7. "My husband and I disagree over how we should relate to our son. Even though we both disapprove of homosexuality, he feels okay having our son and his partner come into our home. I'm very uncomfortable with that and would feel unable to sit down to dinner with them and pretend nothing's wrong. What should we do?"

If you're unable to have your son and his partner in the home without extreme discomfort, then he and his partner will sense it (even if you try hard to conceal it), and everyone involved will have a tense, nonproductive time. So instead of trying to force something that won't work, try making other arrangements.

Since your husband is more comfortable seeing them as a couple, he could visit the two of them together without you, and your son could visit you at home without his partner. (You should be prepared for him to refuse this option, but you can at least ask.) Either way, you'll need to be honest with him about your limitations. Don't apologize for your discomfort—it doesn't make you "wrong"—just explain it and try to negotiate around it.

8. "My gay son attends what he calls a 'gay-friendly' church, where homosexuality is celebrated as a gift from God. My wife and I have invited our son to attend church with us, which he says he'll do, but only if my wife and I also go to the gay church with him. Should we?"

No. Attending a church with someone is a far cry from going to a neutral location with him, such as a restaurant or a park. When you attend a church, you participate in its worship service, which is a clear statement of unity. And if unity isn't there (and in this case it wouldn't be), your participation would be at least dishonest. For that reason, I'd urge you to decline the invitation. Just as your son is clearly entitled to not participate in things he believes to be wrong, so are you. In fact, conscience dictates this.

9. "My daughter has given us an ultimatum: Either we treat her and her partner the way we'd treat any married couple—which means having them stay in our home when they visit from out of town, join all family activities, and be considered a couple like any other—or else she'll cut off all communication with us. We don't want to be bullied into a compromise, but we also don't want to lose our daughter. Should we comply with her demands?"

Your daughter is forcing your hand by demanding something you cannot in good conscience do. First, try appealing to her sense of fairness. Before she came out, she knew where you stood. Ask her plainly, Do you see us demanding that you *reject* lesbianism or we'll have nothing to do with you? If not, then why are you demanding we *accept* lesbianism or you'll have nothing to do with us? It's an unreasonable and somewhat childish demand.

But if the demand stays in place, you have no choice but to refuse and let her do what she feels she needs to. It will no doubt be heartbreaking, but you're being forced to choose between two hardships: the hardship of being estranged from your daughter and the hardship of complying with something that violates your conscience. No one should have to make that choice, but since you must, at least make the choice that does not require you to give in to bullying you don't deserve.

10. "My son claims to be Christian, but his view of the Bible has changed to a much broader, what he calls more 'inclusive,' approach. And his beliefs seem to have changed about many things, not just homosexuality, ever since he came out. Is it possible he is still saved, as he says he is, or has he lost his salvation?"

If salvation really can be lost through ongoing, unrepentant sin, then it's possible he is apart from Christ. But even if that can be the case, so long as he's alive there can also be the possibility of his repenting and regaining the standing before God that he lost.

Another possibility (a strong one, in my opinion) is that, rather than being damned, he's *deceived*. Paul referred to the Galatians as being deceived, yet he didn't suggest they were unsaved (see Galatians 3:1). This seems especially relevant to your son, since his view in general seems to have drifted further and further from biblical moorings. (Remember too that the Corinthian church was a mess—read all of 1 Corinthians to get a clear picture—yet Paul referred to them as the "sanctified in Christ Jesus," indicating that, no matter how far they'd gone into error, they still belonged to Christ.)

So at this point, there's no way to prove conclusively that he's unsaved, or saved but deceived, or saved but backslidden. What you can say for certain is that he's wrong. Why he is wrong, or how his wrongdoing has affected any relationship he may have with God, is something you cannot judge.

Chapter 4

When Your Teen Says "I'm Gay"

*When relationships fail it is usually
because someone chooses not to show up
for the battle.*

—Shannon L. Alder

Until recent years, the teenager who felt attracted to the same sex kept the attractions to himself or herself, for obvious reasons. It would be nearly impossible to find anyone who'd understand, much less affirm, homosexuality. All the main sources of emotional support—peers, parents, siblings, friends, teachers—would disapprove, and many would outright despise and reject the teen who admitted to being gay. Knowing this, most teens chose to hide, which wasn't hard, because even if they did realize they were homosexual, there wasn't much to do about it.

Few outlets for their desires or opportunities to connect with others existed for them, apart from experimentation with friends, which could always be written off as a joke or ignored altogether. There simply wasn't much an adolescent could do that would identify him as homosexual. No Internet to leave a history on, no gay clubs for teens to be seen going to, no texting to be found, no trail of clues to follow. Since there were few ways a teen could express or explore his homosexual attractions, there were likewise few warning signs to parents. Usually, then, the struggle of the teenage homosexual was solitary.

No doubt for thousands of kids it still is. While it's true the country is experiencing an overwhelming shift toward approval of homosexuality, millions of people (and the communities they live in) aren't shifting. So while the scenario above might seem quaint to someone living in metropolitan areas, in plenty of American towns it's still an accurate one. But even in those areas where "gay" and "approval" seldom go together, there are now outlets from outside the community for teens to explore the issue, and encouragement from influential sources to do just that.

The Internet delivers reassurance that same-sex desires are normal and that anyone who says otherwise is ignorant, hateful, or both. It also offers contacts with other homosexual kids, ideas on how to "come out" to family and friends, and assurances from psychologists, professors, scientists, doctors, and even religious figures. And, of course, there's an abundance of gay porn. Television features openly gay sitcom characters, programs hosted by lesbian and gay celebrities, films touting the normalness of homosexuality, and talk shows condemning the traditional Christian viewpoint while extolling the enlightened pro-gay position. And Hollywood's aggressive sanctioning of homosexuality is available at any local theater. All of these sources are there for adolescents pondering whether to resist or celebrate their same-sex attraction.

Then there's the reality of the widespread, institutionalized pro-gay communication offered to students in big-city areas. Public schools advocate for approval of homosexuality, gay-friendly clubs are available on campuses nationwide, openly gay and lesbian teachers serve as role models, gay community centers cater to both youths and adults, and coursework in many states requires the study of homosexuality from a gay-positive view.

Thus we can hardly be surprised at the growing number of junior-high and high-school kids who are considering, deciding on, then announcing their homosexuality. I honestly don't think we have more gay teenagers today than we did before, though that's a possibility. I'm more inclined to think that kids who previously would never have considered openly affirming their same-sex desires are now doing so, as an inevitable result of societal approval and social change.

A change, perhaps, that's making an appearance in your own home. Maybe it's shown itself in an Internet message left on the computer, a text you intercepted, a note you found. Maybe you caught your son viewing gay porn sites or your daughter chatting in an online group for lesbian and gay teens. Or maybe your child simply said, "This is how I feel—this is who I am." However it played out, now you know something about your teenager that you didn't know before. So now what?

"Not My Kid!"

A common temptation among parents who discover that their daughter or son may be homosexual is to presume the kid is simply confused. After all (just for starters), what teenager isn't? How often do they go through phases, trends, dramas, and different forms of self-identification? It's therefore not exactly illogical to figure that when the teen says, "I'm gay," it could really mean, "I'm not sure about these feelings I'm having, so I'm just assuming they mean I'm gay."

Any parent in your position would prefer to think that's the case, rather than consider their girl or boy to be genuinely homosexual. And in fact, that may be the case. Some kids really *do* experience a season of confusion over their sexual makeup. Boys may be curious about their own bodies, comparing their private parts to other boys (even to the point of looking at pornographic images of males just to see how they measure up) and then presume, because of all that, that they must be gay. Or they may, and often do, engage in sexual acts with friends as an outlet for their pent-up hormonal urges. They might also have powerful admiration for a highly masculine boy or man, wanting that person's approval and being fascinated by the person himself. Or maybe the simple friendship and affection of an admired boy will trigger in a teen strong responses aping, but not really being, feelings romantic in nature.

In light of all that, many a boy might seriously question whether his feelings are emotional or erotic, or if the experiences he has had with other guys indicate proverbial teenage "horniness" or long-term orientation. Girls likewise can and often do develop strong feelings for their friends, feelings approaching passion in the level of love and commitment they have for each other. Wondering whether such bonds indicate lesbianism is logical; some girls mistakenly assume *deep* love equals *homosexual* love. So yes, your teen may be more confused than genuinely homosexual. It does happen.

And it doesn't. Often your worst fears are, sadly, confirmed, and the fantasies and attractions your teenager is describing indicate a definite preference for the same sex over the opposite sex. It's tempting to decide for yourself which scenario fits your situation and to tell yourself you know better than your teen what she or he is really experiencing.

But in fact, no one knows better than your daughter or son what your daughter or son feels, and my honest (though not easily given) advice is to take your teen at his word. So the first step, when an adolescent says after careful and extended consideration, "My sexual feelings are strongly and clearly for my own sex," is to recognize that most likely, the kid knows what he's talking about. You by no means need to label him; you're not required to refer to him as "gay," "homosexual," or anything similar. But you should accept what he's saying about his feelings at face value.

If at this point you've not yet read chapter 1, "Now That You Know," and chapter 3, "Loving a Gay Son or Daughter," then please do so before reading further. As a way of building on these chapters, let's look at some specific challenges and experiences common to your situation.

Who's in Charge?

If there were a saying I'd advise parents to repeat to their teens, it would go something like this:

I cannot tell you what to feel

I cannot tell you what to think

I can and will tell you what you may or may not do.

Plainly put, you're still in charge, and now more than ever you need to act like it. But being in charge means, among other things, recognizing what you can and can't control. So when a teen discloses her or his homosexuality, the Christian parent needs to convey these basic points, clarifying what is understood, what is hoped for, and what is expected. Let's break these points down.

"I Cannot Tell You What to Feel"

The first phrase clarifies what's understood, which is that your teen did not choose to feel sexually attracted to the same sex. And if he was unable to decide what his sexual feelings would be, then surely you can't either. It can mean a great deal to a son or daughter to know that Mom and Dad don't hold them responsible for what they cannot do, and one thing a child (or adult) cannot do is simply "decide" to be gay or straight. As mentioned earlier, homosexuality as an orientation is something that is discovered, not chosen. But often a son or daughter will fear that Mom and Dad think they simply chose to be homosexual, and therefore the parents will blame or even punish her or him for desires that the child never did, and never could, choose. Making the statement "I cannot tell you what to feel" shows respect for the involuntary nature of sexual orientation. (Refer to chapter 2, "How Can This Be?" for a fuller treatment of the question "What causes homosexuality?")

It also can open up a terrific discussion on how to handle feelings as a serious believer, as opposed to a nonbeliever. So if your son or daughter is a Christian, this would be a good time to point out the power of our fallen nature, and the fact that because we all struggle with some area of the flesh—lust, pride, sloth—you can appreciate how hard it is to have attractions or urges you wish you didn't have to deal with. You can even point out how poignant this is in the sexual area, because God requires sexual intimacy to be expressed only in the safety of monogamous heterosexual marriage, yet He also allows believers to wrestle with countless temptations to violate that standard.

Here some honesty and disclosure on your part can be helpful. For example, I've heard many Christian fathers tell their sons that while they cannot personally relate to homosexual temptations, they can sure relate to sexual temptations in general. One father I worked with put it so well to his son:

"Okay, I get it. You didn't ask for these feelings. They come up daily—they seem relentless. So join the club! I've been married to your mother thirty-five years, and on a regular basis I have to tear my eyes away from other women. I have to resist the urge to masturbate; I have to watch what comes over my computer. And don't think having a legitimate sexual outlet in marriage cures all of that! My flesh wants a lot more than what I can have, so don't tell me I don't know what it's like to deny feelings that seem so natural and strong."

You don't want to oversimplify this, certainly. Although most of us have to deal regularly with sexual temptations, only a smaller percentage of us know what it's like dealing with temptations outside the mainstream, and controversial to boot. Still, the principle is the same, and this is a good time to point it out. Nobody gets everything they want. Everyone wrestles with desires for things forbidden; nobody is so completely satisfied, sexually or in any other way, that at times illegitimate outlets can't look pretty darned good. Saying no to the flesh is not the exclusive territory of the homosexual, after all.

So yes—you can say with integrity, "I cannot tell you what to feel."

"I Cannot Tell You What to Think"

Nor can you tell him what to think. On this point, you certainly can tell him what you hope for—that he will consider his upbringing, the teaching in your home, and above all his relationship with God and how his decisions will impact that most important of all bonds. That's where you express to him your hope that, in any decision he makes about this or any part of his life, he will first and foremost consider God's will.

That said, you'll probably find it useful to remind your teen that you respect her or his free will, that free will is in fact God given and cannot be overridden, and that you realize she or he needs to decide what her or his position on the matter is.

No small thing, by the way. Because while it's true we do not choose the direction of our sexual feelings, we surely choose the expression of those feelings. On a daily basis we decide to either express or resist countless desires that crop up. The desire to kiss our wife goodbye, the urge to run over the jerk who just cut us off on the freeway, the pull to blurt out something rude and inappropriate when someone offends us during a business meeting, you name it. We decide what our position is on these matters and respond accordingly.

So will your teen. Your hope and earnest prayer is that she or he will make decisions based on biblical truths. But the reality is, decisions good or bad will be made, and even now the kid is deciding what he thinks is true or false, right or wrong, natural or unnatural. You're able to decide what he can do, where she can go, who they can "hang" with, true. But when it comes to what they think and what conclusions they come to, that's another matter.

I suppose you'd give anything to be able to program their minds to land on the right positions, while you realize you've no right or power to do so. So just as it's helpful to clarify that you cannot dictate their feelings, it's also useful to reiterate the obvious: They know what they've been taught about morality; you hope they'll decide to adopt those teachings in their own lives; but you cannot force them to agree with those teachings, much less live according to them, when they reach their own adulthood. You cannot tell them what to feel; you cannot tell them what to think.

"I Can and Will Tell You What You May or May Not Do"

But that hardly means you're going to shy away from telling them what *you* think, or what standards they're expected to live by while under your authority, which leads to the third point: You can and will exercise your authority when it comes to their behavior.

Behavior includes where they go, who they socialize with, what materials they watch or bring into the home, what clothes they wear, and what groups or clubs they join. Clearly, as they age and hopefully mature, we're inclined to give them more leeway in all these areas and more, but at times—and this may well be one of them—a re-evaluation is called for. Examples abound:

- If a teen has been caught using porn on the computer, a filtering device is called for and restrictions should be put around computer usage.

- If a daughter has been in a sexual relationship with another girl, wise parents will insist the relationship end and will not allow their daughter to continue socializing with the girl, just as (I hope) those parents would respond if their daughter had been sexually involved with a boy.

- If a son has joined a gay-support club through his school, his parents have every right to insist he quit and tell him, should he still desire to join such a club as an adult, he'll be free to do so.

- If a teen has been sporting pro-gay buttons, patches, or similar accessories, the parents are entitled to clarify what sort of advocacy he can wear, what sort he can't, and enforce those limitations.

You're aware, as all parents are, that you can't control every part of your son or daughter's life. You cannot dictate who they will speak to at school or who they'll have lunch with, and sometimes a determined adolescent will circumvent whatever limitations have been placed on him. Knowing all that, it's still clear that limitations are called for. In rearing my own sons, I've often had to remind myself that when I stand before God to answer for how I've raised them, I'll be held accountable for the standards I taught and enforced in the home, even if the kids at times sneakily got around them. (Which they sometimes did—but all in all I'd say I've been blessed hugely with dynamic, godly sons, and I've got no complaints!)

A Time to Speak

Initially, the discovery of a teen's homosexuality will lead to clarified terms and policies. Not always, because at times all that has happened is a son or daughter's honest declaration of their sexual feelings. No rules have been violated; no illicit relations engaged in. That sort of disclosure doesn't call for restrictions or new terms. At other times, some things may be limited or cut off—computer or cell phone use, for example—if a teen's behavior has been out of control. Terms will be clarified as needed; expectations as well. But when the dust settles, there's also a time to speak of the questions and concerns you have and to let your son or daughter speak as well.

As you know by now, an adolescent may simply refuse to talk about what's on her or his heart, and all the cajoling, threatening, or pleading you can manage won't crack the wall. When angry, deeply frustrated, or frightened, many teens retreat into their rooms, literally and figuratively, leaving their parents clueless about what's going on inside them. This may be one of those times. And if it is, I don't recommend badgering. But if conversation is still possible (and usually it is), I recommend three primary points to bring up:

1. *"We want to know what this has been like for you."*

So many questions are raised when a teen admits homosexuality: How long have you felt this way? How did you determine you're homosexual? Did you feel you couldn't come to us with this? Has it bothered you keeping this secret, and if so, how? In short, what's it been like for you dealing with this? Asking this shows genuine interest in what she or he has been through, and shows you're not just wanting to lay down rules but are wanting to understand as well.

2. *"We want to know how you feel about homosexuality itself."*

It will help you determine what you're dealing with if you can get your son or daughter to clarify his or her own position on the subject. Certainly, many kids will just tell their parents what they want to hear, so encourage honesty. You're not going to punish them for having an opinion contrary to your own, but you are asking them to let you know what that opinion is, even if you don't like the answer.

Often it will be "I think it's wrong." That means either the teen is planning to resist it, or he's considering giving into it even if he believes it to be wrong. Other times, the answer will be "I'm not sure anymore. Maybe this isn't a sin—maybe it is. I'm still deciding." If that's the case, be sure to affirm the honesty behind that statement, which leads to the next point.

3. *"Where are you spiritually?"*

The fact an adolescent attends church or youth group hardly makes him a committed follower of Christ, and it could be that at this time his spiritual zeal has cooled. Considerably, in fact. Many teens will admit that, after years of "praying against" their homosexuality only to find it still stubbornly present, they get sick of hearing it's such a sin when they know full well it's a tendency they didn't choose. So they feel caught in a classic "damned if you do, damned if you don't" scenario that leaves them questioning the very existence of God or at least the reality of Christianity. So this might be a good time to hear his or her thoughts on faith itself.

The answers to these questions should help you decide what direction you want future conversations between you and your teen to take. If he states he's always felt afraid to tell you about this because he feared your rejection, now's the time to talk about your love for him, your sorrow to hear he was afraid to be honest with you, and your desire for him to let you into this part of his life and be an ally to him.

If she says she's no longer sure whether she believes homosexuality is a sin, this is a good time to discuss how she determines what's right or wrong, how authoritative Scripture is, and what sort of worldview she's adopted.

If he claims he's no longer sure where he stands with God, you might consider having him speak to your pastor or youth minister, or engaging with him in a study of apologetics to re-establish the authenticity of the faith and the need to live in conformity to it.

A Time to Listen and Consider

Sometimes the issues aren't so simple and may go way beyond the scope of sexuality. Some teens are deeply depressed, seriously and even dangerously, not just over their homosexuality, but over the bullying, rejection, and ostracizing they've had to endure from classmates and peers. Because no matter how "gay affirming" the culture seems to become, there will always be kids who brutalize other kids simply because they're perceived as homosexual.

A horrifying rash of teen suicides occurred in 2010, for example, when five adolescents from different parts of the country, some as young as 13, killed themselves, apparently in response to intolerable treatment they were receiving from classmates because of their homosexuality.[1] In most cases their parents were unaware of what they were enduring, so it's entirely possible to have a severely depressed teenager who's facing horrendous pressures and mistreatment, without knowing anything close to the scope and depth of the problem.

If your adolescent seems depressed, then insist she or he be evaluated by a child psychologist who specializes in screening for depression. Do not underestimate the seriousness of the problem, because as is so often the case, what is apparent to fathers and mothers is only the tip of a lethal, tragic iceberg.

This is not to suggest every teen who admits to same-sex attractions should be put into counseling. On the contrary, I have long held the belief that teens should not be forced into counseling simply because they've admitted to homosexuality—because in that case, forced counseling will not only be ineffective, it may well be damaging. And a number of states have passed or are considering laws making it illegal for a licensed counselor or therapist to treat a minor in an attempt to change the minor's orientation or beliefs about homosexuality. But depression or other forms of behavioral or emotional dysfunction should be attended to by a mental-health professional, and their seriousness should never be underestimated.

This is especially true if your teen (or child of any age) is being bullied. By definition, bullying is behavior directed from one party to another in which there is a power imbalance, in physical strength or social standing, for example, which is being leveraged to demean the disadvantaged party.

In plainer terms, it means a kid or group of kids is singling out another kid for verbal abuse, threats, intimidation, humiliation, or physical assault. It can be as simple as a child being loudly called "Fag!" or as horrendous as a student being beaten.

Bullying is never justified; always serious. So if your son or daughter reports being bullied at school you do need to immediately take action by reporting this to your school's authorities and making sure you know specifically what action they will take to protect your child in the future. And if the answers you get are not satisfactory, you'll need to consider other options for your child's education, whether at another school or through homeschooling.

Of course, a student may be reluctant to admit to being bullied, either out of shame or fear of retaliation. But according to the informational website stopbullying.com, symptoms of bullying can include unexplained injuries, lost articles of clothing or personal property (again unexplained), changes in social or living habits, loss of interests in activities that used to interest the child, difficulty sleeping, loss of appetite, or avoidance of school and/or social situations.

If you suspect this is happening to your own son or daughter, you can make it clear that no matter how strongly you oppose homosexuality, you just as strongly oppose bullying and will confront anyone bullying him or her. Ask plainly if anyone is bullying him, get the details, and validate his or her willingness to be honest about this with a clear demonstration of appreciation. Then take action, and immediately. No child should ever have to endure the torment of bullies; every childhood and teen experience should be one which is safe and free of threat.

Five Other Issues Parents of Teens Frequently Ask About

1. "My son says he'll agree not to have sex, but he still wants to go out on dates with a boy he considers his 'boyfriend.' He says if they're not having sex, then he's committing no sin, just as if he were dating a girl but not having sex with her. Is he right? What should we do?"

If you object to homosexuality, then your objection is to all forms of homosexual expression, whether or not they involve genital contact. As parents of a minor, you have the prerogative to decide not only who your son associates with, but what sort of relations he'll engage in. A dating relationship with another boy is in fact a gay relationship, sex or no sex. If you object to your son engaging in a romantic bond with another young man, then you object to this relationship.

Comparing a dating relationship between two boys to that of a boy and a girl misses the point. A nonsexual courtship between a boy and girl is not inherently wrong, and it has the potential to become a legitimate marriage. A nonsexual courtship between two boys or two girls holds no promise of a biblically legitimate union, and it only reinforces feelings and patterns you are telling your son to resist until he is an adult, at which time he can decide for himself what to do with his sexuality.

2. "Our daughter insists she's entitled to go to the Gay–Straight Alliance group at her high school. She swears the group is a main source of comfort and support for her and we have no right to keep her from it. Is she right?"

She is not. The group you're objecting to is one that will reinforce ideas and standards you're in disagreement with. That being the case, you've every right to keep her from it.

I would strongly suggest, though, that you consider how much the group may have come to mean to her. That's not to suggest allowing her to continue with it; rather, it's only to point out that for her, your refusal to let her continue may feel like a crushing blow. She may well have found, for the first time, levels of empathy and camaraderie she's never experienced before, and now you're taking it all away. I honestly believe you should because no parent should allow a child's participation in a group the parent simply doesn't believe in. But as you disallow it, make sure she knows that you're aware of how deeply she feels for the group and that you're not making this decision lightly. Remind her she'll soon be able to decide for herself what groups she'll align with, but for now, it will have to be your decision.

3. "My son seems depressed, and we want him to see a counselor. He says he'll only go to a non-Christian counselor because he doesn't want to be told homosexuality's a sin. What should we do?"

If your son is depressed, you want him to get the help he needs, whether it comes from a Christian or non-Christian mental-health professional. I don't say that lightly, because I'm well aware of how much influence a therapist or counselor may have, and I would always prefer my own loved ones receive counsel from people who themselves receive counsel from God. But if he refuses to see a Christian therapist, rather than trying to force a counseling relationship he's not open to, I would suggest locating a secular therapist, meeting with him privately to discuss your situation, and clarifying to him your position as a Christian and your desire for him not to undermine your positions. If he is willing to respect your values and not contradict them during his work with your son, he may well be able to help him deal with his depression, and some real benefit could be gained.

4. "Our daughter has lesbian friends at school who she swears she's not sexually involved with, and we believe her. But we're still concerned because of their beliefs and behavior."

There are plenty of ways kids influence each other without sex being involved, so any parent in your position would feel concerned. The bottom line is that you have the right to scrutinize and, at times, limit your daughter's friendships and associations. This goes beyond sexuality and really is a basic premise. If you are not comfortable with the kids your daughter hangs out with, you have the right and responsibility to intervene and restrict as needed.

5. "Our teenaged son has admitted his same-sex feelings, but he refuses to discuss the subject any further with us because he's certain we do not and cannot understand. 'You just don't get it,' he keeps saying. Should we try to force the issue, or leave it alone?"

In a way he's right, and there's nothing wrong with admitting it. You cannot fully know what it's like to wrestle with homosexuality unless you've done so yourself, and since you probably haven't, then he has a point. But, as mentioned earlier in this chapter, you surely know what it's like to wrestle with feelings and desires, so to a point you definitely can relate to him, and you should tell him so. Likewise, you should emphasize to him how unfair it is to cut you off just because he's experiencing something you don't personally relate to.

That said, there's a time for dropping the subject. So long as your teenager is complying with boundaries you've set down and is in other ways basically functioning as he should, I would recommend calling a moratorium on the subject. He knows where you stand; he knows what the rules of the house are. If you keep belaboring the issue, you may well close down all communication, which you surely don't want to do.

So admit to him that no, you don't fully understand, but you'd like to, and you'd love it if he'd help you understand by describing what this has been like for him. Promise to listen without interrupting (and of course, keep that promise!), and make sure he knows you appreciate his letting you in a little deeper. You're not going to change your standards or home policies, but you can certainly try to understand what his experience has been like, and you can make sure he knows you want the bond between you to stay intact regardless of your differences on this issue.

Chapter 5

When Homosexuality Hits Your Marriage

*Your own feeling tells you that you were not what
you are. That which promised happiness when we
were one in heart is fraught with misery now that we
are two. I have seen your nobler
aspirations fall off one by one.*

—Charles Dickens,
A Christmas Carol

When you vowed "I do" for better or worse, you thought you knew what "worse" meant. Now you realize it can actually mean *unimaginable.*

But then, who really understands the immensity of marriage vows? All of us who say them make an earnest but uninformed promise, reciting words like "sickness" and "poorer" without, in most cases, having experienced severe forms of either. Marriage is honorable, of course, and for most people it's desirable. But it's also a leap of faith.

In your case, it's landed you in completely unknown territory. You assumed "for worse" meant something bad, but something you could at least relate to—maybe a quick temper, or sloppiness you didn't see when you were dating, or laziness, or poor spending habits. You might even have thought he could lose sexual interest in you at some point, or that you'd have screaming matches or periods of silent hostility. In other words, you always knew you'd have problems, but you assumed they'd exist within boundaries, and one of those boundaries was heterosexual. When the problems go beyond those boundaries, it's like seeing a movie switch genres midstream.

When you're watching a Western movie for instance, you expect the plot to develop within certain guidelines. You know conflicts will come—saloon fights, train robberies, shootouts—but you expect them to exist within the cowboy framework. So if a spaceship suddenly appears in the middle of the film, you'll be completely taken aback, unprepared for an element that's not supposed to impose itself on a Western.

So it is when homosexuality hits a marriage. It's a spaceship landing in the middle of a Western—something you knew existed in other films, but which could never (you thought) make an appearance in *yours*.

Yet it has, and now that it has, you may be wondering why you didn't see it coming. No one can know precisely how many heterosexual women have unsuspectingly married homosexual men, but the number is large—and for every deceived woman, the effect can be devastating. Clearly, a spouse's homosexuality is not easily predicted. And in your case, as with many others, the warning signs may have looked like virtues, not red flags.

His sensitivity, for example, may have seemed to be one of his best qualities. When you began dating, he displayed good listening skills and a high level of empathy—rare features in men! Being on a date with him may have felt like being in the company of a caring, concerned girlfriend who had unusual insight into you and your feelings.

And he was a gentleman. You observed early on that, while he was affectionate and warm, he seemed anything but sexually threatening. His expressions of affection didn't go too far; you never felt you had to stop him from physically "crossing the line," and you assumed that was a sign of respect and godliness. So when comparing him to other men you'd known, maybe you decided this made him a refreshing exception to the rule: attractive, sensitive, considerate, gentlemanly, and thus a very good catch.

Only now, in hindsight, does another picture emerge: The sensitivity that was so attractive may actually be a temperament commonly found in gay men—good communication skills, vulnerability, easily expressed emotions—making you wonder now if they are assets or liabilities. And the lack of sexual aggression, first seen as a desirable trait, is now just a lack of normal sexual interest, which is anything but flattering. After all, you wanted a lover for a husband, not a considerate male roommate.

Or maybe, as is sometimes the case, there really were no warning signs. Maybe your sexual relations had always been fulfilling, your communication honest and productive, your life together good. Then slowly, almost imperceptibly, the façade unraveled.

The Picture Emerges

When the revelation of homosexuality comes about, it usually occurs in three stages: *absence, secrecy,* and finally *discovery*.

1. Absence

In the absence stage, nothing seems overtly wrong. It's insidious. You dated, made promises, and began a life together without major conflict. But then a lack of certain things—passion, deep talking, regular time together—showed there was an absence within the marriage.

Willa Medinger, wife of ministry leader and former homosexual Alan, describes this period:

> The first two years of our marriage were ideal…Then life became hell for Alan and me. He was unable to give to me at any level.[1]

Mary Ann Hastings, married to a man who struggled with homosexuality, recounts,

> We settled into a comfortable marriage. We loved each other, shared many mutual interests, had bright career

possibilities...After six months, however, Lance became depressed. I felt uneasy, like I was being warned of a coming crisis.[2]

Usually, it's nothing on the surface. Instead, it's a general decline in the deeper parts of marital life: sexual relations, intimate talking, time spent together. And usually, much as a wife in these cases will implore her husband to tell her what's wrong, he'll insist things are fine—meaning, of course, he's not ready to address the problem.

2. Secrecy

Absence leads to secrecy, one of the worst poisons that can be introduced into a marriage. Secrecy begins when a spouse starts keeping vital information to himself—information that could, if brought to the light, be dealt with and resolved (developing a secret habit of using pornography, for example, or masturbation fantasies). But the shame so often accompanying homosexuality keeps many women and men from facing it, so it remains hidden, unconfessed, unchecked. At this point, it may seem like the homosexual spouse is simply a liar, bent on deceiving and using an innocent partner.

Yet my experience with married men and women who are attracted to the same sex tells me they don't intend to deceive their spouses in most cases. They marry because they truly love their partners and believe firmly, if naïvely, that their homosexual temptations will pose no future risk. (A common remark I hear in counseling is, "I really felt that, once I found the right partner, my homosexual temptations would go away for that reason alone.")

The shame over this particular temptation is often relentless and also contributes to the secrecy. Most of my clients have been Christians who believed not only that homosexuality was a sin, but that no one—not even their future mates—could accept or understand that homosexual temptations were part of their everyday struggle.

And sometimes, especially in cases of lesbian women I've worked with, the struggle didn't seem to be much of an issue until they'd been married for years. Only after marriage did a strong attraction to a particular woman occur, usually in the context of a deeply emotional relationship.

So the most common response I get to the question "Why didn't you tell your spouse about this *before* you got married?" is either, "Because I loved her, wanted to be her husband, and thought she'd never have me if she knew about *this*," or "I loved him, and even though I'd had feelings for women in the past, I didn't think *this* would be an issue once I bonded with him."

So *this* stays hidden, sometimes for years, leading to secrecy. The secrecy begins in earnest when the occasional homosexual temptations a husband or wife has been feeling become desires they're now flirting with or indulging. Maybe the indulgence comes through pornography, maybe an anonymous encounter, maybe an emotionally dependent relationship with a friend or even a fellow church member. He or she crosses the line and then, devastated, covers it up rather than confessing it. And thus an emotional, shame-based wall is erected.

Adding to the problem is the innocent spouse's awareness—if through nothing but instinct—that the wall is there. But until the spouse who has put up this wall admits it (and its cause), the innocent spouse can't prove there's a wall. She can only plead, question, or nag, all of which is usually met with denial, leaving her convinced *she* is the problem.

3. Discovery

Finally, and inevitably, comes discovery. When it comes, it is first and foremost an answer to prayer, as God hears the cry of a bewildered spouse. He sees the lonely partner wondering what went wrong in her marriage and why she's so alone and seemingly unloved. He watches the confused husband reaching for a wife who seems increasingly remote, hoping to find a way to her heart, which now seems so closed. God sees, and in time He intervenes. That's when discovery occurs.

Sometimes it occurs because the spouse involved in homosexuality is simply tired of the secrecy and, in the interest of integrity, comes clean. Other times—in my experience, most of the time—discovery comes because the spouse has been found out by his or her partner. The partner may find evidence of Internet pornography or gay/lesbian-oriented websites or a letter to a lesbian lover or a receipt from a hotel the husband used for a tryst. However it comes, discovery brings the problem into the light, provoking an enormous crisis. But it is only through such a crisis that the marriage has any chance of surviving.

If this is where you are—if you've recently made the discovery your spouse is attracted to the same sex and may have been acting on those attractions—let's begin with the questions and issues you may be dealing with.

Be clear about this, first and foremost: You have *nothing* to do with your spouse's homosexuality or with his or her decision to indulge it. You didn't create the problem—it existed long before you ever met your partner. And you've done nothing to make your spouse's desires for the same sex increase, nor have you had anything to do with your partner's decision to act on those desires.

You are *not* the problem; you did not *create* the problem; you are not *responsible* for the problem.

But you've inherited it, all the same. That being the case, you've got work to do to protect both yourself and your family. And the first order of business is to make sure you've got resources to help you and guide you.

Establishing Your Base

Before working on the marital aspects of this problem, you've got to gather some personal resources. Two things in particular are essential: counsel and allies.

You need *counsel* from someone who understands your situation. After all, if you'd been defrauded financially, you would seek counsel from an attorney to learn what your recourses were and what you could expect to recoup. And if you'd been in an accident, you would seek counsel from doctors, auto specialists, and insurance agents.

In your case, you've suffered both: You've been cheated (perhaps to a great extent), and you've sustained an injury. So you need guidance from someone with experience in injury and recovery. Make an appointment—*today*—with either your pastor or a Christian counselor. Tell him you've recently discovered your spouse is involved in homosexuality, and you're reeling both from the discovery and from the myriad of emotions it's raised in you. Then allow this person to walk with you through the long process of healing and restoration of both you and (hopefully) your marriage.

Along with getting professional help, develop some *allies*. Allies are friends or associates who know what you're going through and who offer their support and encouragement as you go through it. You can find allies either among your *existing friendships,* or your *family,* or a *support group* for people in your situation.

Allies among your existing friendships. You might pick two or three women whom you trust and feel close enough to confide in. Your message to them is, in essence, "I've just found out my husband is attracted to men. He's been using porn/meeting men/involved in an affair, and I'm crushed. I really need someone to talk to while I'm figuring out what to do; someone who can cry with me, grieve with me, pray with me, and encourage me—or at least listen. I just don't want to go through this alone. Can you go through it with me? Can you keep it confidential? Can I lean on you?"

Friends are invaluable, especially when you're grieving and in crisis. But be careful to confide in only the few you trust and feel comfortable discussing it with and who are mature enough to keep the matter confidential.

Some make the huge mistake of telling their entire circle of friends about a partner's sin. Sometimes this is done without malice; sometimes it's done deliberately as a way of punishing and humiliating a partner. But in all cases, it backfires. It strikes a permanent blow to a marriage that's already in crisis, puts the friends in an uncomfortable and awkward position, and makes the person doing the disclosing look, ultimately, bitter and divisive. Avoid this mistake. It's costly, and once it's been made, it cannot be undone.

Allies among your family members. In lieu of friends, you may choose to go to family members. A parent or sibling can be a great comfort at this time, and I see no reason not to go to family members, provided your relationship with them is close and you feel they can handle this information without jeopardizing their future relationship with your spouse.

So if you can lean on family members, so much the better. But make sure they're willing to accept your partner in the future, even with the knowledge of what's happened. Remember, if your marriage survives (and in most cases, it will), then you and your spouse will want a continued relationship with your family. If you feel that disclosing the homosexuality will endanger that relationship—if, for example, they'll hold a grudge against your partner long after you've offered forgiveness—then look elsewhere for support. In the long run, you'll save the entire family a good deal of grief by doing so.

Allies among a support group. You may feel there's no one in your family or your circle of friends you'd feel comfortable talking about this to. (That may indicate a social problem you really need to look at—but at a later time.) But if for now you don't know who can be an ally, you might look into Christian support groups for spouses of homosexuals.

These groups will provide a forum, usually weekly meetings, at which you can get feedback, encouragement, and solidarity with others who share your experience. And often they're genuine lifesavers. (For more information on support groups, check the "What to Do Now" section in the back of this book.)

In addition to counsel and allies, you'll need to take stock of and care for your personal, emotional, and spiritual health. Look again at the section in chapter 1 headed "Depression," in which I outline some basic steps to take during this period of grief. Put these in place now before addressing the problem further with your spouse. Then, having done so, you need to determine what to do about your marriage.

And much of what you decide to do will be determined by your spouse's actions and intentions. More specifically, you'll need to determine if your husband or wife is rebellious, resistant, or repentant.

The Spouse in Rebellion

He is, as the word *rebellion* suggests, unwilling to abandon the sin he has brought into the marriage. So when it's discovered, he'll defend it, protect it, or blame you for it.

Having been found out, he may tell you that he's glad, because he needs to finally accept who he really is. He may have already read materials telling him homosexuality is inborn, normal, even ordained by God. Then, armed with this information, he sees himself as an innocent victim of a homophobic church and society. He married (he says) innocently believing that was the thing to do. But now, after trying to be a husband, he cannot and should not deny his true feelings. So he'll yield to them, allowing you to find another partner, because he cannot go back to denying himself.

By now he may have withdrawn from your church or his old Christian friends, knowing they'll never go along with this line of thinking.

In fact he may have developed a whole new set of allies who encouraged him to come out and who'll reinforce his new prohomosexual beliefs. He may express real anger at the church (some justified, some exaggerated) and minimize the basics of the faith, choosing instead a doctrine of self-fulfillment and self-gratification.

Your lesbian wife may also be angry with you, and as always there may be good reason. But with the anger may also come an unfair amount of blame. She may blame you entirely for the state of the marriage or her ungodly behavior or even her decision to marry you in the first place. (It's amazing, really, how a person in rebellion can find evidence of guilt in everyone else.) And while it's true you've been less than perfect and might indeed have a lot to repent of, you can never be blamed for another person's willful and disruptive sin.

Overriding all of this, in the case of a rebellious spouse one fact will become tragically clear: Your partner will not take responsibility for his or her behavior and has no intention of giving it up.

The Resistant Spouse

He will, in contrast to the rebel, admit homosexuality is wrong. He'll apologize when found out, fully admitting how wrong his actions are, then he'll make promises, ask forgiveness, and want to move on.

What he *won't* do is examine what led up to the problem. Nor will he take steps—such as seeking counseling, joining a support group, or reading appropriate materials—to help ensure the problem won't just go underground for a while, only to reappear in the future.

A resistant spouse is a master at minimizing. When found out, he generally makes it sound as though his sin is a minor slip, human and common, and not worth all the fuss. If pornography has been his outlet, he'll say he has only used it a few times, or he was just curious. If he has had actual contact, he'll understate its importance ("It was only once," "I really didn't enjoy it," and so forth) while insisting he won't repeat the offense, and so further action is unnecessary. When you want a fuller explanation as to why this happened, or mutual counseling, or some sort of prevention plan, the resistant spouse will pull out Christian clichés: "You're not forgiving me," or "It's under the blood and needs to stay there," or "I've claimed victory over it." The desired effect of this resistance is to make you seem to be lacking spirituality.

The resistant spouse isn't a rebel, nor does he *intend* to repeat his sin. But since he won't agree to deal with it, the chances of relapse are very high indeed.

The Repentant Spouse

This husband echoes the prodigal son's attitude when he returned to his father. The son had sinned; he had few expectations. He only wanted to be forgiven and received, and he was willing to accept a lesser position in his own home in light of what he'd done.

So the repentant spouse will show willingness to do two vital things: take complete responsibility for his actions, and take any steps necessary to prevent a repeat of those actions.

He'll have a certain tenderness born of failure and humility. He won't justify his behavior, nor will he minimize it. He'll willingly attend counseling, groups, or pastoral meetings, and he'll answer your questions (and you'll have many!) forthrightly and without defensiveness. He won't expect you to simply "get over it," since he realizes it will take time to rebuild marital trust. And he'll accept that, just as he'll accept the challenge to win you back with his actions, not just promises.

Your Response and Action Plan

1. If you've discovered your spouse's behavior but haven't yet confronted him, plan to do so as soon as possible. If you're uncertain what to say or how to say it, make an appointment with a pastor or counselor today and plan the best time and approach. Then follow through. You cannot allow this to remain a secret in your marriage.

2. If you have discussed your spouse's behavior and the problem is out in the open, determine immediately if your partner has put you at risk for HIV (the AIDS virus) or other sexually transmitted diseases.

If you're *certain* the behavior has only involved noncontact activities (such as using pornography or Internet chat rooms), then you're not endangered. But if you are in any doubt as to whether or not he's told you the truth, or if he has admitted to being sexually active with other men, then you need to be tested immediately. Abstain from sexual relations now, and make it clear that you will be tested and that you'll need him to do the same before you can resume them. Make an appointment with your physician and be honest about the reason. Be tested for HIV and other sexually transmitted diseases, and follow your doctor's guidance to the letter.

3. If you have children and they do not know the specifics of the problem, do not discuss this with them. Telling them at this point puts an unnecessary burden on them.

4. If your spouse is rebellious or resistant, determine, with the help of a pastor or counselor, under what terms you're willing to remain in this marriage. This is not a suggestion to divorce or separate; rather, I'm recommending you draw boundaries and *then* determine what you'll do if they are not honored.

I've found that rebellious spouses, if they're going to repent, normally do so only when they realize their behavior is going to cost them what they hold most dear. So let your partner know that unwillingness to abandon this behavior and work with you on restoring your marriage will bring into question the future of the marriage itself. The boundaries you draw should include

- separating from the behavior or person involved (for example, if it's been Internet pornography, you expect your spouse to get a new Internet Protocol (IP) address and hard drive—which probably means a new computer—and the latest filtering software—to which you will have the passwords—or else do away with the Internet altogether; if it's a relationship with an individual, you require total severing of all communication with that person)

- joining you for marital counseling to determine how your marriage is to be preserved

- seeking help from a pastor, counselor, or ministry specializing in help for repentant homosexuals

These boundaries should be nonnegotiable. Determine beforehand what action you'll take—temporary separation, for example—if they are not honored.

5. If your spouse is repentant, give assurance of your support, but emphasize that trust and forgiveness are two different things. You can decide to forgive; your trust will have to be rebuilt. Insist on the steps in point 4, then apply yourselves to rebuilding.

As you do, you'll find the rebuilding is not done only in your spouse or your marriage. It also becomes a new, abundant season for you.

Kathy Gilmore, at the time cofacilitator of Metanoia Ministries (a ministry to repentant homosexuals) in Washington, said this of her own process after learning of her husband's homosexual encounters:

> On my own, I could never have done what God asked of me—I can't save myself, let alone my husband or anyone

else. But Jesus lives His life in us. We become the flesh that carries out His will. In February of 2001, Paul and I celebrated our twentieth wedding anniversary. He is a new man; I am a new person, too, because I have learned to allow God's love to live in me.[3]

When the smoke has cleared and the heartache is resolved, may you be able to say this as well.

Ten Other Issues Spouses Frequently Ask About

1. "I've decided to be tested for HIV. If I've been infected with the virus, will it show up immediately? How long does it take for the virus to show itself? And if I have been infected, does that mean I will definitely get AIDS?"

    You should be tested, but don't be anxious about too much too soon, because the situation is often not as dire as it seems at first.

    According to the Centers for Disease Control, the test for HIV is actually a test for the antibodies your system produces when it's been exposed to the virus. Most people develop detectable antibodies within two to eight weeks (the average is 25 days); 97 percent develop antibodies within three months of exposure; in rare cases, it can take up to six months. That means it takes a maximum of six months to know for certain if you're infected.

    If your husband has been sexually active with other men, then both of you need to be tested *now.* Then, after your test, wait six months and be retested before having sexual intercourse, to make certain you've allowed the maximum amount of time for the antibodies to appear. If they don't and if you're certain your spouse has had no contacts during the six months, then you should be safe in resuming intercourse.

If you are infected, that by no means guarantees you will develop Acquired Immune Deficiency Syndrome (AIDS). Many people who are HIV positive never develop this syndrome. But, of course, you need to discuss this in detail with your physician. There are many treatments available for people carrying the virus, and many live long and healthy lives. So again, while it's hard to resist, do not jump to conclusions at this point.

2. "My wife had an affair with another woman. She's come clean about it and has cut off all ties with her. But she swears that, before this affair, she was never attracted to women and that she really isn't a lesbian. Can this be true?"

It can. For a number of reasons, many women are drawn into unhealthy, deeply emotional relationships with other women. At times, these can become sexual, even though the emotional element is, in these cases, the strongest component. And many women who have engaged in lesbianism find it to be more of a phase or an isolated event. (With men, homosexuality tends to be more of a long-standing problem and is hardly ever simply a phase.) That being the case, it's entirely possible that your wife is telling the truth, since it has been true of many others.

3. "My children heard my wife and me arguing when she first found out about my behavior. They know something is wrong, and they know it has to do with me and with sex. You said children shouldn't be told about this, but in my case, they already know at least part of the problem. Should I tell them the rest?"

Yes, since it's better not to leave them in the dark. First, discuss this with your wife and be sure you both agree on what you're going to disclose. Then meet with your kids and tell them, in your own words, the following:

"I know you've heard your mother and me arguing, and I know you know something very bad has happened. This is what's happened—I broke a very important promise I made to your mother. Now she's hurt and angry, and we have a lot of work to do to make it better. But we're going to do everything we can to make it right, and we want to make sure you know how much we both love you and how much we both want to protect our family. So I promise you we'll do that. And if you have any questions, I want you to ask them. Don't worry about me or Mom getting embarrassed—just ask whatever's on your minds."

Let them be the ones to ask for specifics. They may not realize you committed adultery, so don't push that information on them. But answer their questions honestly and completely, and with each answer, remind them that you're going to try to make it right.

4. "My husband had a relationship with another man, which he says he has broken off, at least sexually. But he says this man has also been a good friend, and he wants to retain that friendship without sex. I'm very uncomfortable with this and want him to stop seeing this man altogether, even as a friend. Who's right?"

You are. It would be very naïve of you to allow this friendship to continue, and it shows bad faith on your husband's part to want to continue a relationship that has caused you so much pain. Make sure he understands that even if the relationship is no longer sexual, it's a source of fear and pain to you, and as his wife, you expect him to value your feelings above those of this other man. Let him know that by no means is such a relationship acceptable, and that unwillingness on his part to completely discontinue it will be a major stumbling block to your marriage's future.

5. "My husband has repented of homosexuality but says he still has strong attractions to the same sex. Does this mean he's not really

repentant, or is there something more he should be doing? Can he ever really change?"

If a man has been primarily attracted to other men for most of his life, then to some extent those attractions will remain, even if and when he develops strong attractions for his wife as well. Remember, sexual response is deeply ingrained and, in most cases, involuntary. In other words, he did not choose to be attracted to men. He only chose whether or not to act on those attractions. Since that's the case, he cannot simply choose to *not* be attracted to men. In fact, to some extent he will probably have to resist those attractions for the rest of his life.

So what can you realistically ask for and expect? You can expect him not to indulge attractions to men when they occur. You can expect him, specifically, to abstain from masturbation, pornography, or any sexual outlet outside of marriage.

That doesn't mean he can't have a normal and fulfilling relationship with you, both emotionally and sexually. But like all men, he will at times have to deal with temptations and attractions toward someone other than his wife. And like all men, he'll have to remember that just because a wrong attraction is present, acting on that attraction is never a legitimate or acceptable option.

6. "If my husband has been using gay pornography, does that constitute adultery? If so, am I justified in filing for divorce?"

   Since the divorce question is one of the most contentious issues modern Christians face, you'll hear several different responses to this question. Let me give you mine, but first let me strongly suggest you discuss this with your pastor and carefully search your conscience and weigh your options before making such a drastic decision as divorce.

Having said that, my opinion is that using pornography does *not* constitute adultery and, for that reason, does not constitute biblical grounds for divorce.

Remember that when Jesus compared lust to adultery in Matthew 5:28, He stated, "I say to you that whoever looks at a woman to lust for her has already committed adultery with her *in his heart*" (emphasis added). He later declared, in Matthew 19:9, "Whoever divorces his wife, except for sexual immorality, and marries another, commits adultery."

By combining these two Scriptures, some have assumed Jesus meant that a spouse's adultery is just grounds for divorce, *and* that lust, even without action, constitutes literal adultery, so lust alone is grounds for a husband or wife to file for divorce.

Yet Jesus made a distinction between adultery of the heart and literal, physical adultery. Both are sins to be sure, and both should be taken seriously. But the consequences of the two are different, as should a spouse's response be.

Compare this to what John wrote in his epistle regarding murder. In 1 John 3:15, he declared, "Whoever hates his brother is a murderer." Here John clearly says there are two different types of murder: literal and internal. Both are serious, but our response to each is different. No reasonable person would suggest the death penalty be applied to someone who hates, even though hatred is a form of murder. The two are clearly different—I, for one, would much rather be murdered in someone's heart than literally killed!

So it is with adultery. Adultery of the heart is a grievous sin, but to count it the same as physical adultery—a literal sexual encounter with another person as opposed to lust or sexual fantasy—is, to my thinking, as absurd as counting hatred the same as the literal killing of another human being.

Having said this, let me add that I have at times strongly advised a wife to separate from her husband because of his ongoing use of pornography. Children are endangered by this material because they may well find their father's porn or walk in on him as he's viewing it. And the man who uses it insults his wife and defiles his home. So if he refuses to abandon it, the wife may have no choice but to have him leave the home. Again, though, this constitutes temporary separation, not divorce.

7. "I understand that adultery may justify divorce. But what about separation? When, if ever, is separating a good idea?"

Review the descriptions of the rebellious, resistant, and repentant spouses in the earlier part of this chapter. If your spouse is rebellious—that is, refuses to separate from homosexual contacts or the use of pornography—separation may be a good way of allowing some time to consider what he or she is throwing away. It may also give you some space to consider whether or not to stay in the marriage, and it will give you some room to heal. In my opinion, those are all good reasons for a separation.

Another good reason to separate may be to heal the wound you've sustained as a result of your spouse's behavior, even if he or she is repentant. If, for example, your spouse had relations outside your marriage, you may continue to feel violated by being under the same roof, and you need—maybe desperately—to be alone for a time. In that case, separation may be useful.

Be certain, though, that you don't use separation as a tool for punishment. Rather, it should be a way of taking time apart from each other to determine the future and direction of your marriage. And of course, the decision to separate should *not* be made without counsel from either your pastor or a professional Christian counselor. Be sure that there's a rationale for your separation and that it includes clear terms: length, terms of contact and visitation, and goals (what you hope to accomplish by separating). In other words, if you do separate, do so with a redemptive purpose in mind, rather than as a knee-jerk reaction to a painful situation.

8. "My wife says that when we make love, she still catches herself thinking about a former female lover she had. Even though I believe my wife has truly repented of this, it sickens me to think of her still longing for someone else when she's with me. Should we discontinue all physical relations?"

No, since that would be conceding the victory to evil: to your wife's fantasies over your marriage. If she has been honest enough to admit this to you, she's showing integrity. You need to honor that by working with her on this rather than walking away.

Of course, the pain of knowing she still thinks about someone other than you is intense, and there's no reason to apologize for feeling as you do. But beyond that, talk to her, especially when you're being physical, and try to keep the focus on the two of you in the here and now. Remember, the brain records any intense experience we've had and stubbornly reminds us of those experiences, often at the most unhelpful times. Don't hold this against her. Ask her to resist those memories, pray together about them, and work together on building what you have without dwelling on what threatened your marriage in the past.

9. "My husband says I've been too pushy and bossy in the past, and that has made it easier for him to yield to his homosexual tendencies. I say this is a cop-out and he's got to take responsibility for his own sin. Am I wrong?"

Technically, no. Your husband is the only one responsible for his behavior, and you cannot be blamed for that. But if you have been, as he says, bossy and pushy, then you have sins of your own to repent of. Of course, they did not create his sin. But nonetheless they are sins, and I often find that the spouse who has committed sexual sin is assigned the "villain" role in the marriage while the other spouse's sins are ignored. So if you've been too aggressive or dominating, you have indeed made it *easier* for him to sin, although you did not *make* him sin. There's a difference. So by all means insist that he take responsibility for his behavior. But fairness requires that you ask the same of yourself as well.

10. "What is my role in my spouse's recovery from sexual sin?"

   Your role remains what it has always been: to be a life partner, lover, co-parent—all the roles wrapped up in the concept of "spouse." You are not, however, your spouse's counselor, pastor, parent, accountability partner, or official nag. In other words, let your spouse use the proper resources for recovery: a godly accountability group, a pastor, a counselor, and so forth. You be what you agreed to be from the beginning—nothing more, nothing less. That's enough work for anyone.

Chapter 6

When Other Family Members Are Gay

*I've missed you. I never dreamed
our beliefs would separate us.*

—Inherit the Wind

When your child or spouse is homosexual, you're affected in ways only a parent, husband, or wife can be. The trauma is deep and all-encompassing, and you need to make very hard decisions about the relationship and the future.

When homosexuality hits home in other ways—when the gay loved one is a sister, brother, uncle, nephew, parent, or in-law—the pain can also be deep, and along with it come any number of questions and concerns. So if one of your immediate or extended family members is gay, this chapter is for you. In it, I hope to address the situation, answer your questions, and equip you to deal with a difficult but not at all impossible situation.

Let's begin with you and how the news of your family member's homosexuality has affected you, both *emotionally* and *circumstantially*.

The Impact on Your Emotions

When a loved one is gay, your feelings are obviously going to be impacted. And as always, the closeness or lack of closeness between you and this person will determine how deeply your emotions and situation are going to be affected.

For example, a Christian musician came out as lesbian after years of music ministry with her sister in a well-known singing group. The two had been close, so the older sibling's homosexuality had tremendous impact on the younger one, leaving her to cope with extraordinary pain and the challenge of maintaining a relationship without offering support for a way of life she could never condone. In this case, both *emotions* and *circumstances* were deeply affected.

In another case, a young man I consulted with heard through the family grapevine that his older brother was gay. They'd hardly spoken over the years, having had some bitter fights and rivalries. Even so, this brother was emotionally affected by the news of his sibling's homosexuality. He disagreed with him on moral grounds, but unlike the two sisters mentioned above, there was hardly a relationship to preserve or negotiate. So while his *emotions* were affected, his *circumstances* were not.

In yet another family—a well-known one, in fact—neither emotions nor situation were impacted to any real degree. In 2001, a distant nephew of the Rev. Jerry Falwell came out publicly, making an issue of his blood ties to one of America's most visible critics of homosexuality and even posing nude for a gay publication, saying, "So, Uncle Jerry, whaddya think of this?"

As Falwell hardly knew the young man in question, he was, predictably, unfazed. He must have been disappointed to see a family member display himself so brazenly, but neither his *emotions* nor his *circumstances* were seriously impacted by the actions of a distant family member with whom he'd had little or no contact.

Emotional closeness, then, determines emotional impact. The closer you are to your gay loved one, the more your emotions and circumstances are affected.

Emotionally, if there's been a bond between the two of you, that closeness is now broken. You've lost the certainty that the two of you pretty much agree on the basics. You've lost confidence in the openness of the relationship since you now know there's something this person kept from you, maybe for years, when you thought you knew him or her so well. You've lost unity, perhaps, as this issue now divides you. Even though you love this person so much that you want to maintain all you've had, you realize he or she is going in a different direction, one you can neither condone nor relate to. And seeing that directional change may be one of the toughest losses you're facing.

If the two of you haven't been close, emotions are still involved, but they don't run as deep. In cases like this, my clients normally report feelings of uncertainty or discomfort. "What," they ask, "should I say, if anything? Do I even have the right to comment on this, since we've never known each other that well?" As Christians they may feel challenged to witness to this gay relative, but they often wonder where or how to start a conversation about eternal issues. Meanwhile, there are family gatherings to deal with, Christmas cards to write or not write, and weddings to attend or decline (see chapter 8 for more about your approach to same-sex weddings). Even when there's been little or no bonding, even a distant relative's homosexuality can evoke an emotional response.

History also plays a role in your feelings about a gay loved one, so what's happened between the two of you *before* you knew about the homosexuality has much to do with the way you're responding now that you *do* know.

So the son of a gay father—a young man I've known for years—had an unusually hard time dealing with his father's homosexuality, not only because he felt homosexuality was wrong, but because his father walked out of his life so early. It was a common scenario: young Christian man with homosexual tendencies marries Christian woman, keeping his sexual desires for men a secret. He eventually begins indulging in homosexuality, forms a relationship with another man, then leaves his wife and young boy. The son never knew the real cause until later in life, by which time he felt abandoned and betrayed by his father. Naturally, homosexuality wasn't the only, or even the main, problem. A history of silence and misunderstanding stood between them.

History also played a role in the bitterness I saw between two sisters, both of whom were raised in the faith, and one of whom had joined a pro-gay church, having become a lesbian activist. Because they had been so close, when the one came out, both felt betrayed and enraged by the other's reaction. The lesbian sister felt judged and snubbed by her sibling and resented her for not understanding homosexuality. The straight sister felt equally betrayed by her sister's decision and her unwillingness to reconsider it. Because of their history, both were extremely tied to each other emotionally. They couldn't help but be profoundly affected by the rift.

So at this point, you're dealing with an emotional response to your loved one's homosexuality based largely on your closeness to and history with that person. If you're experiencing real loss—if the two of you have been close and you're sad, angry, or confused—then go back to chapter 1 and reread the section headed "Depression." Take the actions I've recommended there. Allow a normal grieving process, increase intimacy with God, make use of pastoral or professional care, and make sure you are taking care of yourself overall. You'll need to speak with your gay family member as well, but before you do, put these steps in place.

The Impact on Your Circumstances

Your family circumstances—how you relate, how often you see each other, and on what terms—will also change to some extent. These changes don't need to be severe and shouldn't spell the end of the relationship. But they will call for adjustments. The time you spend together, the topics you discuss, the issues you either argue about or avoid—all of these and more—will need some fine-tuning.

So to adjust your relationship fairly and lovingly, to whatever extent it needs adjusting, get *clarification* from your family member, both as to positions on homosexuality and feelings about your relationship. Then *express* both your desires for the relationship and your position on sexuality.

Building or Rebuilding Your Relationship Through Clarification

When you clarify, you're trying to ascertain two things about your gay loved one: the status of your relationship, and where the person stands on homosexuality. Both are important. It will be hard, after all, to have a productive conversation about the subject if you don't know how your family member feels about it. And it will be harder still to even broach the topic without knowing how comfortable this person is speaking to you about a very personal subject.

1. Clarify the Status of Your Relationship

Now, please don't ask a family member, "So…what is the *status* of our relationship?" That sounds awfully pretentious and stuffy. But since that is what you're trying to determine, come up with an engaging way to ask.

So whether the two of you have been very close or distant, if you want to build or rebuild your relationship, a good way to begin is by asking for some clarification about *us* (as in "I'd like to talk about this—are you okay with that?" and "Homosexuality aside, are *we* okay?") and about homosexuality itself.

Let me offer a few examples of how this could be accomplished under various relational circumstances. Any of these sample exchanges could take place via e-mail, telephone, or in person.

If you and this family member have been close, the relationship is still good, and you're in the habit of talking about personal issues. Remember: He probably already knows you disapprove of homosexuality, and he feels some discomfort with that. He truly doesn't want to hurt you, but he also doesn't want to be preached to or have to keep this part of his life hidden from you. In many ways he's in as much of a quandary as you are.

Clarification: "I've just been told (or you just told me) you're gay, and I want to talk about it. Can we talk honestly? We've always been close, and whatever you decide to do with your life, I want to be sure we stay close. So how about it? Is this a subject I can ask questions about and speak freely about? If so, great. But please tell me if I'm crossing the line. I want to respect you and your feelings even if we disagree. And I hope we can work out ways to protect our relationship, no matter what our beliefs are."

If you and this family member have *not* been close, although there's been no hostility or rift between you; you've just never known each other very well. Remember: Since the two of you haven't been close, she may not even know you hold a traditional view on sexuality. Or if she does know that, she may assume you're very judgmental and insensitive, so her defenses may be up. Thus, as soon as she hears from you she may well be asking herself why you're contacting her and what your real purpose (or "agenda") is.

Clarification: "I've heard you're homosexual, and even though I know we haven't been too close in the past, I really would like to talk with you about this.

"But I also don't want to barge in and assume I have the right to discuss something so personal with you because, without your permission, I don't. So what would you think about meeting and talking about this face-to-face? I have so many questions and concerns, and you probably have a good deal to say too. I can tell you up front that I take a pretty traditional view on human sexuality, but I also take a dim view of people's treating each other disrespectfully. So I promise in advance to respect your right to make your own decisions and not to push my views on you. And I'm hoping we'll find ways to have a respectful, maybe even closer, relationship in the future. If you can join me in this advance agreement, can we talk?"

If you and this family member have *not* been on good terms, and you feel you've wronged him in some ways. Remember: He probably still feels hurt over your shared history, and that clouds his ability to hear you when you talk about love and concern. In fact, he may have been waiting for years for you to finally address this, and he may wonder what's prompting you to address it now.

Clarification: "When I heard (or when you disclosed) that you're gay, I thought of two things: First, how I feel about homosexuality, but then—and maybe more important—how uncomfortable I feel about my actions in the past. There are things I've said and done I know were wrong, and it would mean so much to me if we could meet face-to-face so I can apologize and try, if possible, to make it right.

"I'd also like to talk about the gay issue, although you may or may not be open to that. If you're not, I won't push it. But if it's something we can discuss, I have some real concerns and questions. You probably have a good deal to say too. So can we talk about that as well? Whatever decisions or understanding we come to, I hope we'll be able to reconcile, and I hope we'll maintain a better relationship in the future."

If you and this family member have *not* been on good terms and you feel personally wronged by her over long-standing problems the two of you have had. Remember: There's a good chance she still feels guilt or regret over the past and wonders if you're going to seize this opportunity to confront or even attack her. She may also have a very different take on what's happened between the two of you, so be certain you listen to her side of this, for you may find you've been holding on to a very unnecessary and unfair grudge.

Clarification: "I know we haven't been close in the past, but I've been thinking about you, your being gay, and the way our relationship has been up to now. There are things between us I've never really talked about: hurts from years ago, problems we've never really looked at, and some areas in which I really do feel you've been wrong. But you may feel the same about me, so we both may have long-standing issues we need to discuss.

"Can we do that? I'd like to be honest with you about my feelings, and I promise to respectfully listen as you tell me yours.

"As for homosexuality, I'd like to discuss that as well, although you may not be open to that. If you're not, I won't push it. But if it is something we can discuss, I have some real concerns and questions. You probably have a good deal to say too. So can we talk about that too? Whatever decisions or understanding we come to, I hope we'll be able to have a frank and respectful talk, and I hope we'll maintain a better relationship in the future."

Your primary goal at this point is to establish whether or not you and your loved one are both ready and willing to discuss question of homosexuality. Such a discussion would include understanding how your family member feels about homosexuality and how he or she intends to live. It will also include an expression of your own feelings and position on the matter and a discussion of the terms under which you're going to continue in relationship.

If your family member is *un*willing to discuss this, then you'll need to move on to chapter 7 and develop whatever boundaries or terms will be necessary in the future. But if discussing this is an option (and it usually is), then you need to get a fuller picture of this person's perspective on sexuality.

2. Clarify His or Her Beliefs and Intentions

When you have your discussion, your first general question might be, "Have you decided this is normal and moral, or are you still deciding? And on what basis will you make, or have you made, this decision?"

When someone says, "I'm gay," that doesn't answer the question as to how the person feels about homosexuality and why. In other words, two questions are primary: Has the person truly decided he's attracted to the same sex, and is he (or she) what we'll call "gay-affirming"? *Gay-affirming* means holding a belief that homosexuality is normal and legitimate. So "I'm gay" can mean any of the following:

1. *Decided and gay-affirming*: "I'm gay, that's fine with me, and I'm waiting for the rest of the family to finally accept it."

2. *Undecided*: "I'm attracted to the same sex, but I'm not sure whether or not it's okay to act on these attractions. I'm still deciding, but I at least want to be honest about the existence of these attractions."

3. *Decided but not gay-affirming*: "The attractions are definitely there, but I know homosexuality is wrong so I don't intend to act on them. I intend to resist them."

To get a better understanding of where your relationship is headed, ask which of the above best describes him or her. After listening carefully, then you can act as follows:

1. *If he is decided but not gay-affirming*: That means he is, in essence, admitting that homosexuality is a *temptation*, but he's also rejecting it as a *way of life*. Offer your wholehearted support and appreciation for his honesty. Make sure he knows you're aware of how hard it is to say no to something the rest of the world seems to be saying is normal, and reassure him he has an ally and friend in you. If he's unaware of resources to help him

keep his commitment to purity, refer him to the organizations and books listed in "What to Do Now" at the back of this book.

2. *If she is undecided*: Ask candidly on what basis she will be making her decision. Scripture? Her feelings? Professional or academic opinions? Don't ask with the goal of challenging her answer—make it clear you only want to better understand how she will come to one of the most momentous decisions she'll ever make.

Ask if she's open to talking to a Christian counselor or pastor whose viewpoint may be more traditional and who can offer a different perspective than the one she's probably been hearing. If she consents, refer to the resources listed in the back of this book.

But if she prefers not to, I strongly suggest you not push it. I've seen too many families pressure their loved ones into counseling, with predictably bad results. If you push her into a counselor's office, I can almost guarantee you that you will not only *not* get the desired results, but she'll resent you deeply for the intrusion.

3. *If he is decided and gay-affirming*: Ask what, if anything, he's expecting of you. Agreement? Discussion? Conversion to his way of thinking? Again, the goal here is not to start an argument but rather to get a better idea of his expectations. This will help you clarify your own position and negotiate the relationship from here on.

3. Clarify Your Own Position on Homosexuality.

Don't beat a dead horse by repeating, every time you see your gay family member, what the Bible says and why you disapprove of homosexuality. That's unnecessary. But make certain you've clarified, once and for all, where you stand. I find it helpful to use the five points mentioned in chapter 2 when articulating reasons for objecting to homosexuality.

Yet they don't include all that needs to be said at this point. Let me also suggest you make sure your gay loved one knows the following:

- You know he or she didn't ask for these feelings.

- You appreciate his or her honesty.

- Your position on the matter is still unchangeable.

- You want to protect your relationship through mutual respect and, as much as possible, mutual understanding.

- You may never agree on this issue, but you're committed to not letting that disagreement ruin your relationship.

At this point, you will have clarified three things: whether or not your family member is open to discussing this issue with you, where he or she stands on it, and where you stand as well. That does not, of course, answer the question about how you'll be relating in the future. That topic will be addressed in the next chapter.

Ten Other Issues Family Members Frequently Ask About

1. "My sister has told me she doesn't, at this point, want my parents to know about her lesbianism. She's asked me to keep it to myself, but is that the right thing to do?"

   Assuming your sister is an adult, then yes, you should respect her wishes. It's up to her when and how she tells your parents about this. But you should also point out to her that it does put a bit of a wedge between you and your parents and that you hope she'll tell them soon because you don't like keeping secrets from them.

   However, if your sister is a minor, I do feel your parents should know, and you would be in the wrong to keep this from them. As her primary caregivers and guardians, they have the right to know something as crucial as this. So I would suggest you tell them now and let your sister know why you couldn't in good conscience comply with her request.

2. "My brother was raised Christian, and he claims that even though he's gay, he's still a believer. I don't want to cut him off, but when I read in 1 Corinthians 5:11 that we should not have anything to do with a Christian who's living in open sin, does that apply to family members as well?"

In 1 Corinthians 5:11 Paul says, "I have written to you not to keep company with anyone named a brother, who is sexually immoral, or covetous, or an idolater, or a reviler, or a drunkard, or an extortioner—not even to eat with such a person."

I'm convinced this Scripture does *not* apply to family members. If it did, it would mean Christian husbands and wives would have to literally stop living together if one of them drank too much, raged, or showed evidence of idolatry. Likewise, it would mean Christian children would have to refuse to be in the same room with their Christian parents if those parents were involved in such sins. And obviously this would all contradict other Scriptures commanding us toward family harmony. So while I do believe we are commanded to withdraw from a believer (but not a blood relative) who is committing such sins, I do not believe these verses compel us to withdraw from our own family members.

3. "My aunt and her partner are adopting a child. What role, if any, should I and the other family members play in this?"

Your aunt is in sin; the child involved is not. (An out-of-wedlock pregnancy, for example, produces a child under the wrong circumstances, but the child itself could hardly be considered wrong and should be welcomed and cared for.)

That being the case, this child deserves all the love and support you can give. By all means be involved in the child's life to the fullest extent your aunt will allow. No matter the circumstances behind this child's birth, it is—as is all life—sacred and precious.

4. "Our brother has come out to us. We have younger children, and they love their uncle very much. Should we tell them about him, and if so, how should we tell them?"

At some point, yes, you'll need to tell them. So ask your brother to let you be the one to do so, because you want to determine when and how this is disclosed.

Judge the timing for this as you would judge the timing for discussing any sensitive subject with your kids—determine their level of maturity and trust your instincts, much as you would with the "sex talk." (It's hard to say at what age kids in general are ready for that, either, but your instincts are a pretty good guide.)

Then, when you feel they're ready, include the following points when you tell them about their uncle:

- You love him very much, you always will, and you hope they always will too.

- Their uncle has decided he's gay. You don't approve, and you're praying he'll change his mind about this, but for now this is what he's decided.

- You're not going to compromise your beliefs, and you won't ever allow anything to be practiced or expressed in the home that violates your moral principles.

- As much as possible, you want to keep the family together. You're not sure at this point how this will affect the family's future, but that will largely depend on what you and their uncle can agree on when it comes to family visits and policies.

- You'll answer whatever questions they have as honestly as you can. If they need to talk with a counselor or pastor about this, you'll make an appointment for them.

- You want them to be honest with you about their feelings. If they're angry, confused, or upset, you want them to feel comfortable talking it over with you or with their uncle, if he's open to that.

Then let your brother know you've had this talk with your children. Emphasize that you hope his relationship with them will stay close, but make sure he understands the need to respect your teaching and boundaries in the home, especially regarding your younger kids.

5. "My husband and I disagree over how we should relate to his sister and her lover. Even though we both disapprove of homosexuality, he feels okay having them come into our home. I'm very uncomfortable with that and would feel unable to just sit down to dinner with them and pretend nothing's wrong. What should we do?"

If you're unable to have them in the home without extreme discomfort, then they'll sense it (even if you try hard to conceal it), and everyone involved will have a tense, nonproductive time. So instead of trying to force something that won't work, try making other arrangements.

Since your husband is more comfortable seeing them as a couple, he could visit the two of them together without you, and your sister-in-law could visit you at home without her partner. (You should be prepared for her to refuse this option, but you can at least ask.) Either way, you'll need to be honest about your limitations. Don't apologize for your discomfort—it doesn't make you "wrong"—just explain it and try to negotiate around it.

6. "My gay brother attends what he calls a 'gay-friendly' church, where homosexuality is celebrated as a gift from God. My wife and I have invited him to attend church with us, which he says he'll do, but only if my wife and I also go to the gay church with him. Should we?"

No. Attending a church with someone is a far cry from going to a neutral location with him, such as a restaurant or a park. When you attend a church, you participate in its worship service, which is a clear statement of unity. And if unity isn't there (and in this case it wouldn't be), your participation would be at least dishonest. For that reason, I'd urge you to decline the invitation. Just as your brother is clearly entitled to not participate in things he believes to be wrong, so are you. In fact, conscience dictates this.

7. "My sister has given the rest of us an ultimatum: Either we treat her and her partner the way we'd treat any married couple—which means having them stay in our home when they visit from out of town, join all family activities, and be considered a couple like any other—or she'll cut off all communication with us. I don't want to be bullied into a compromise, but we also don't want to lose her. Should we comply with her demands?"

Your sister is forcing your hand by demanding something you cannot in good conscience do. First, try appealing to her sense of fairness. Before she came out, she knew where you stood. Ask her plainly, Do you see us demanding that you *reject* lesbianism or we'll have nothing to do with you? If not, then why are you demanding we *accept* lesbianism or you'll have nothing to do with us? It's an unreasonable and somewhat childish demand.

But if the demand stays in place, you have no choice but to refuse and let her do what she feels she needs to. It will no doubt be heartbreaking, but you're being forced to choose between two hardships:

the hardship of being estranged from your sister, and the hardship of complying with something that violates your conscience. No one should have to make that choice, but since you must, at least make the choice that does not require you to give into bullying you don't deserve.

8. "My uncle claims to be Christian, but his view of the Bible has changed to a much broader, what he calls more 'inclusive,' approach. And his beliefs seem to have changed about many things, not just homosexuality, ever since he came out. Is it possible he is still saved, as he says he is, or has he lost his salvation?"

If salvation really can be lost through ongoing, unrepentant sin, then it's possible he is apart from Christ. But even if that can be the case, so long as he's alive there can also be the possibility of his repenting and regaining the standing before God that he lost.

Another possibility (a strong one, in my opinion) is that, rather than being damned, he's *deceived*. Paul referred to the Galatians as being deceived, yet he didn't suggest they were unsaved (see Galatians 3:1). This seems especially relevant to your uncle, since his view in general seems to have drifted further and further from biblical moorings. (Remember too, that the Corinthian church was a mess—read all of 1 Corinthians to get a clear picture—yet Paul referred to them as the "sanctified in Christ Jesus," indicating that, no matter how far they'd gone into error, they still belonged to Christ.)

So at this point, there's no way to prove conclusively that he's unsaved, or saved but deceived, or saved but backslidden. What you can say for certain is that he's wrong. Why he is wrong, or how his wrongdoing has affected any relationship he may have with God, is something you cannot judge.

9. "What's the best way to witness to a gay family member?"

The question presupposes two things that are almost certainly wrong. The first is that there's a special way of sharing the gospel with homosexuals, one that's essentially different from the way it should be shared with heterosexuals. Not true, of course—the gospel message is the same for all, homosexual and heterosexual alike. The second presupposition is that there's one best way to share the good news, when in fact there are many good ways and many different circumstances to consider.

The first thing to consider is whether the family member in question is unsaved (having never been born again) or backslidden (was once in close fellowship to God and the church but has walked away) or deceived (thinks he's in good standing before God even as he practices overt and unrepentant sexual sin).

If he's unsaved, start from ground zero—discuss fallen human nature, universal sin, the work of the cross, the gospel invitation. Take into account the misunderstanding many homosexuals have about Christians, though, and realize he may assume you think he's the *worst* sort of sinner. (That's one of the most common perceptions gays and lesbians have about Bible-believing Christians.)

So emphasize the helpless state of all people, no matter what their orientation. Admit that the love of Christ has not always been evident in His people's attitude toward homosexuals.

If he's backslidden, ask why, and ask what his life apart from Christ is like. Is it really better? If not, why not return to Christ? And if he's deceived himself into attempting to marry homosexuality and Christianity, take some time to better understand pro-gay religious arguments; then, if and when the opportunity comes, have an honest—if somewhat confrontational—discussion.

(For a much fuller response to the question of what the Bible really says about homosexuality and how to discuss the biblical position on the matter, please refer to my book *The Gay Gospel?: How Pro-Gay Advocates Misread the Bible*—Harvest House, 2006.)

10. "When it's all said and done, I really don't want to argue with my gay relative. She knows where I stand, after all, and she seems settled in her way of living. And I really like her! So am I wrong in not pursuing this discussion further, or is it okay to just hang out with her, as I always have, without trying to convert her?"

It's not only okay to simply enjoy the company of someone you love; it's a pretty good idea! As you said, she knows your position, so continuing to harp on it will only turn her away. I like the way the apostle John put it in his letter: "Let us not love in word or in tongue, but in deed and in truth" (1 John 3:18).

Your continuing to love her and relate to her in spite of your differences is in and of itself a strong witnessing tool, which her heart continues to hear long after her ears may have been closed to your words. And why shouldn't you enjoy her? Provided she's not asking you to compromise your beliefs or participate in anything you're uncomfortable with or feel to be wrong, there's no reason not to continue to build on the bond the two of you have.

I know this to be true from both personal and professional experience: When Christian family members continue to love and, as much as possible, relate to their gay loved ones, the impact on those loved ones' hearts cannot be measured. It's often unseen, but it broods quietly—maybe for years—until at some point, the heart softened by a family's ongoing, unconditional love becomes prepared for repentance and eternity.

And all because someone said, "It's okay to still love you, isn't it?"

Chapter 7

Negotiating Family Boundaries

*Many sincere, dedicated believers struggle
with tremendous confusion about when
it is biblically appropriate for them to
set limits. When confronted with their lack
of boundaries, they raise good questions.*

—Henry Cloud and John Townsend,
Boundaries

Of all the questions I'm asked by parents and family members, the most common is, "Where do we draw the line?" The question is raised by a variety of situations, such as when a son or daughter wants to bring a lover home to meet the family or join in holiday celebrations

- when a family member wants a gay relationship to be treated like a marriage
- when a teenager wants to join an on-campus gay-support group
- when a gay family member wants to "educate" the rest of the family on the normality of homosexuality

When families face these and other challenges, the "Where do we draw the line?" question has to be asked. So, in this chapter I'd like to try to answer it. While doing so, let's remember the rule we adopted in chapter 2: Where the Bible is adamant, be adamant; where the Bible is silent, be open-minded.

So where does the Bible say to draw the line? That's not so easily answered. To begin with, there are no specific verses telling you under what circumstances, if any, you should adopt this or that policy toward your gay family member. So when there are not specific *verses* to guide our decisions, we look to biblical *principles*. And even on this issue there's considerable disagreement.

I've heard some Christian teachers say, for example, that the principle of unconditional love should be the overriding one. They insist you show love by having your son and his partner in your home, loving them unconditionally—never judging, always accepting.

I've heard others say the principle of standing for righteousness should take priority, and that under no circumstances should you allow a gay family member's partner in the home, as this may give tacit endorsement to homosexuality.

While both these principles are important, I'm convinced neither one works for every family. So instead of adopting a policy that forces a choice between inclusion or exclusion, let me offer a different framework using the principles of *conscience* and *comfort*.

Letting Conscience and Comfort Guide Boundary Making

The *principle of conscience* means this:

> I cannot participate in something I don't believe in, nor can I directly or indirectly encourage another person to sin, since that makes me a partaker of his sin.

I draw this principle from four specific scriptures:

> Judge not, that you be not judged (Matthew 7:1),

in conjunction with

> Have no fellowship with the unfruitful works of darkness,
> but rather expose them (Ephesians 5:11).

and

> Neither be partaker of other men's sins (1 Timothy 5:22
> KJV).

Taken together, these scriptures clarify that, while I cannot judge another person, I can and must judge *behavior*. And if I judge a behavior to be wrong, I have to make sure I'm not participating in it or condoning it. Moreover,

> Whatever is not from faith is sin (Romans 14:23).

If I'm not sure whether a certain situation would constitute my condoning another's sin, my doubt about it tells me to avoid it.

The *principle of comfort* means, in essence,

> I have the liberty to say no to something I'm *uncomfortable*
> with, even if I don't feel the situation, not the homosexual-
> ity, is inherently wrong.

Three scriptures help me understand this principle:

> All the tax collectors and the sinners drew near Him to
> hear Him. And the Pharisees and scribes complained, say-
> ing, "This Man receives sinners and eats with them" (Luke
> 15:1-2).

This reminds me that Jesus associated with sinners while by no means condoning their sin. Thus it's permissible to interact with people of all sorts. So I can, if I choose, enjoy the company of a gay friend or loved one without condoning their sin.

> As much as depends on you, live peaceably with all men
> (Romans 12:18).

I can and should strive for peaceful relationships even with people I disagree with. But only as much as is possible, since in some cases, a peaceful relationship is an impossibility, and I'm not obligated to try to force it.

> Walk in wisdom toward those who are outside (Colossians
> 4:5).

I need to use case-by-case wisdom when dealing with nonbelievers or believers who are compromised, since a lack of wisdom on my part can disrupt relations and dishonor the gospel.

Now, to get a better idea how these work, let me apply these principles of conscience and comfort to a few situations my family and I have faced.

When Conscience *Was Violated*

When I left the gay community in 1984, I did keep some friendships with gay men and women I loved and wanted to stay in touch with. We knew we had differing views on homosexuality and agreed to disagree without letting the disagreement destroy our friendship. This didn't violate my conscience, since we didn't meet in gay bars or clubs, and I was in no way condoning homosexuality by being with them. I had made my position clear, so there was no misunderstanding as to where I stood. I was also comfortable with them. They were my friends; I respected and enjoyed them, so the issues of conscience and comfort were both satisfied.

All was well until two of them asked if I'd attend a ceremony at the gay church in which they would formalize their relationship. (At the time, no one was talking about same-sex marriage; these were just called "unions.")

Now my conscience was jeopardized. It was one thing to meet at a neutral location for lunch; joining them for a union ceremony was another. Attending a gay church would have been a way of stating I was in fellowship, not just friendship, with them. But fellowship implies unity of belief and purpose, which we didn't have. So pretending to be in fellowship would have violated my conscience.

More important, attendance at a ceremony means you approve of the event and celebrate its meaning. I could no more in good conscience attend a gay union than I could attend the wedding of a man who callously dumped his wife for a younger woman. In both cases, my standing with them would have been the same as saying, "I endorse and support this." Since I couldn't do that in good faith, according to the conscience principle, it would have been wrong to attend.

I explained all this to my friends, and sadly, that was the end of our relationship.

When Comfort *Was Violated*

At other times, I've been uncomfortable with some associations even though I didn't think they were inherently "bad."

I remember, for instance, a party to which some old friends invited my wife and me (we were engaged at the time). Most of the people at this gathering were openly gay, but we didn't feel that alone meant we shouldn't attend. It wasn't a "wild" group by any means—just a quiet afternoon pool party with lunch and games.

But as Renee and I mingled with the others, several of the men in the group started questioning us about who we were and why we, a straight couple, were there. When the host discreetly informed them I had been a member of their community who had "walked," they started badgering us with insults and accusations of being homophobic, bigoted, and generally stupid.

Obviously we were uncomfortable. It didn't violate my conscience to be there, but I saw no reason to put my fiancée and myself through this sort of treatment. We excused ourselves at the earliest chance and made a point of declining future invitations from this group.

When Conscience and Comfort Were Clearly Not *Violated*

Other situations have been happier. Years ago, my family and I were neighbors to a lesbian couple. Shortly after we moved into the neighborhood, we got to know them and genuinely liked them. And while we knew we differed on social issues, we developed a good rapport. This wasn't just an attempt at ministry. These women were good neighbors—friendly, considerate, and responsible—thoroughly likable.

So my wife and I were very comfortable with them, and they were with us as well. They would occasionally attend school performances our kids were in and visit for coffee or dessert afterward. Around our kids, they respected our beliefs by never discussing homosexuality or making any overt displays of affection. Likewise, we respected their beliefs by not pushing our views on them, and the result was a solid, comfortable relationship. In fact, when they moved away a few years back, my wife and I felt a keen loss, and to this day we regard them highly. Our friendship with them violated neither our conscience nor our comfort.

Five Family Situations That Illustrate the Principles of Conscience and Comfort

If you apply the principles of conscience and comfort, I think you'll find them useful guides. Let's look at situations you're likely to face and see how the principles of conscience and comfort can help you negotiate and establish boundaries in your home.

To do this, we'll take five common family situations, look at how they impact conscience, comfort, or both, and then offer a response to each.

Situation 1: **A gay family member wants to bring his partner home** for the holidays and sleep in the same room as any married couple would.

- *Problem*: This violates *conscience*. Although having the two of them in your home would not *necessarily* compromise your stand on homosexuality, hosting them in a sleeping arrangement would because it would make you an encourager of the sexual aspect of their relationship.

- *Suggested response*: "You know where I stand on sex. If you had a girlfriend you wanted to bring over, she'd be welcome, but not as an overnight guest in your room. This is no different.

  "I know you view your relationship as a marriage, but I can't in good conscience share your view. I wouldn't ask you to countenance something in your home you didn't believe in; I hope you'll show me the same consideration."

Situation 2: **A gay family member wants to bring her lover to the home** or to a family gathering without spending the night.

- *Problem*: This may or may not violate *conscience*. If you feel you are not openly condoning homosexuality by simply having them as your guests, then there's no problem of conscience. But if you feel that having them over as a couple seems like a statement of your approval, then your conscience will be violated. And no one but you can make this decision.

- *Suggested response* when compromise is possible: I've known cases in which families had their son's or daughter's partners join them for family occasions, and it worked well because, through some negotiating and boundary setting on both sides, terms were made clear:

If children were present, the gay couple would refrain from any form of physical affection or any reference to their relationship as being anything more than a friendship. They would not have to lie, but they would also agree to not volunteer anything by word or action that would identify them as a "couple." (Some refer to this as a "don't ask; don't tell" family policy.)

No family member would be allowed to make denigrating remarks about homosexuals, and the subject would be brought up only if all parties involved were comfortable discussing it. Family members would agree to refrain from pressuring or "preaching to" the couple.

Everyone involved would speak and act in ways that showed mutual respect and sensitivity to one another's feelings and viewpoints.

In these cases, family events were generally pleasant, though everyone involved needed to compromise. The gay couple compromised by not being as open in their words or affections as they normally would be; other family members compromised by not expressing their disapproval of homosexuality no matter how strongly they felt it. Yet no one involved felt his conscience was being violated by this arrangement.

• *Problem*: In other cases compromise cannot be agreed upon. Sometimes a gay couple will simply refuse to act like anything but a couple. They'll insist they should have the right to hold hands, refer to their relationship and, in general, not have to adhere to a "don't ask; don't tell" policy. And as strongly as I disapprove of homosexuality, I can see their point. They feel their own consciences are being violated by having to pretend they're something they're not.

This creates an impasse of course, so family gatherings won't work. After all, if Christian parents allow a gay family member and his lover to express their relationship openly around children, those parents will have a hard time explaining to the kids how they can object to homosexuality yet let it be openly expressed in the home. So for the sake of all involved, when this sort of impasse is reached, family gatherings including the son's or daughter's partner should probably be avoided.

- *Problem*: In yet other cases, even though the gay family member agreed to the terms set above, other family members felt such discomfort at the thought of a family gathering where homosexuals were present that they decided to pass. It wasn't because they felt being with their gay loved one and his or her partner violated their consciences; rather, because they were so uncomfortable with the whole situation, they knew the evening would be strained and tense. That too is a legitimate reason for saying no to such events.

- *Suggested response* if conscience or comfort is violated: "I really am sorry, but I can't feel right in having you and your lover join us as a couple. I'd feel I was saying yes to something I don't believe in, and I really don't think you'd want me to violate my own principles even if you disagree with them. If you'd like to come alone, I'd love to have you, and I really want to see you. But if you really need to bring your partner, I'm sorry, but we'll have to pass."

Situation 3: A gay family member wants to talk openly during family gatherings about his homosexuality or issues surrounding gay rights.

- *Problem*: This may violate *conscience*. Of course, if all family members present are adults, you may feel no violation of conscience, and the discussion may be of real benefit. But if there are children present who you would rather not have as part of this conversation, then conscience will obviously become a problem.

- *Comfort* may also be violated. Not necessarily, of course: If you want to discuss the issues and feel the discussion is mutually respectful, then comfort isn't a problem. But if you feel you're being preached to or pressured, then comfort is violated, and you'll need to draw the line.

- *Suggested response* if conscience or comfort is violated: "We'll need to discuss this another time, as I don't think it's appropriate for the kids to be party to this sort of conversation. I'll have to decide if and when I feel they're ready to know about your sexuality, and I need you to respect that."

- *Or*: "We all know where you stand, and you know our position as well. But since we're not going to change each other's minds, let's not alienate each other by having an ongoing argument. I don't want to feel pressure in my own home to defend my beliefs, and I certainly don't reserve the right to pressure you. So let's operate with mutual respect."

Situation 4: A gay family member simply wants to join the family gathering without making her sexuality an issue (no partner or discussion on sexuality involved).

- *Problem*: Virtually none. Conscience is not violated, since there's no request to compromise or accommodate, nor is comfort, as there is no demand being made that should elicit discomfort.

- *Suggested response*: Welcome and enjoy your family member.

Situation 5: Your teenager declares he's gay or is found to have been viewing gay porn or to be involved in a relationship with another boy.

- *Problem*: Of course, conscience is going to be violated if you take no action. Since as a parent you're responsible for your teenager, you cannot allow him to be involved in something that clearly violates your beliefs. And while you cannot dictate behavioral boundaries to an adult son or daughter, you can and should dictate them to a teenager.

- *Suggested response*: "I can't tell you what to believe or feel, but your behavior is something I do have a say in. If you come to feel homosexuality is normal when you're an adult, then it will be your decision to live as you please. I hope you'll make the right choice. But for now, understand this: If you feel attracted to the same sex, that's beyond my control. Likewise, if you feel there's nothing wrong with being attracted to the same sex, that too is something I can't stop. But your behavior—in other words, what you do about those attractions—is another matter.

  "So, in practical terms: You won't have access to the Internet if I have reason to believe you're using pornography, visiting gay chat rooms, or any Internet site condoning homosexuality. You won't be joining any club or organization promoting homosexuality. And under no circumstances will I condone a relationship between you and another boy.

  "As for your feelings: I love you and am very concerned that you feel you're gay. Maybe you are; maybe you're not. Believe me, it's too early to be slapping a label like that on yourself. But I would like you to speak to a counselor about this if you're willing. If not, I'll let that be your decision. At any rate, for now you'll have to understand this will never be acceptable in my home." (See or review chapter 4, "When Your Teen Says 'I'm Gay,'" for an in-depth treatment of this situation.)

A variety of other family situations may arise. If so, contact your pastor or a Christian counselor to help you negotiate your terms and boundaries using the conscience and comfort guidelines. And remember, when drawing and negotiating boundaries, try as much as possible to preserve the relationship without violating your own conscience.

In most cases, this is not only possible—it's likely to be successful. Then, having laid the framework of boundaries and terms, you're likely to have ongoing discussions about different issues related to homosexuality and gay rights. Chapters 9 and 10 help clarify those issues so you can successfully pursue love and truth in your ongoing family relationship.

First, though, let's address one more boundary, which deals with a situation that occurs more and more often—when you receive an invitation to a same-sex wedding.

Chapter 8

Same-Sex Weddings: "I'll Be There" or "Sorry, Cannot Attend"?

I cannot and will not cut my conscience to suit this year's fashions.

—Playwright and author Lillian Hellman

Until recently, when homosexuality hit home the main challenge to family members was to determine how they'd interact with their lesbian or gay loved one. There was seldom any pressure to be directly involved in anything that validated homosexuality itself.

No more. As same-sex marriage has become part of the law in state after state, growing numbers of Christian family members are not only being told "I'm gay," but they're also being asked to attend a wedding ceremony affirming—celebrating, in fact—a gay or lesbian union. So whereas in the past the pressing question was, "Should we have them over for dinner?" now it's "Do we RSVP 'Yes, I'll Be There' or 'Sorry, Cannot Attend' on their wedding invitation?"

To avoid ambiguity, let me say at the outset that I don't believe it's right for a Christian to attend a same-sex wedding ceremony, even if the ceremony is for a family member. I point this out now to keep the reader from skipping ahead to see what my bottom line is and, more importantly, to keep my own position clear. I am troubled by the lack of clarity from many teachers and authors on this subject, so I hope to avoid the very thing I criticize in others. I'll also point out that there are Christ-centered, sincere believers, some of them prominent, who would thoroughly disagree with me, so viewpoints on the question of attending same-sex weddings differ, even among conservative Christians who believe homosexuality to be wrong.[1]

Let me also say this is no easy issue. What's easy is to hold a position you never really have to live out, making it a snap for many Christians who'll never receive such invitations to huff, "Well, *I'd* never consider going to a homosexual wedding! It's just wrong, and that's that."

Well, yes, but it really isn't a matter of, as some say, "that's that." There are ramifications we should consider and prepare for, helping us not only to arrive at the right position, but to hold that position with a full understanding of its impact and the sacrifice it might require at times.

A Wedding from Your Loved One's Perspective

In Shakespeare's *Romeo and Juliet*, Romeo complains of his friend Mercutio that "he jests at scars that never felt a wound." In other words, he makes light of something he himself has never experienced. That's a sin of omission in my book, a lack of empathy brought about by unwillingness to try seeing the other person's viewpoint. And while I want to maintain biblical integrity and clarity, I likewise don't want to be casual about the feelings of others, even as I disagree with them and in some cases have to make decisions I find necessary, even if they find my decision hurtful. And the decision not to attend a loved one's wedding qualifies as one of those tough ones.

Try looking at it from the perspective of the person being married. First, she or he is no doubt in a relationship that's very serious; most likely, very committed. To have reached a point of considering marriage, both parties involved have probably thought the issue through, considered the way they feel about each other, weighed the nature and value of their relationship, and decided to form a union they hope will last a lifetime. Yes, by biblical standards, the union is wrong; the wedding itself a ceremony solemnizing something that in God's sight cannot be called a marriage. But to the couple involved (and to your loved one in particular, be that loved one a child, sibling, cousin, or even parent), it's dead serious, a joyful milestone they're anticipating and wanting to share with the people they love the most.

Yes, they probably know you are a Bible-believing Christian who doesn't condone homosexuality. But they're also hoping that, despite what you believe, you'll put that aside for the sake of sharing their joy, supporting them in love, and in essence being there for them because of who they are to you. For your loved one, this is a life-changing event, one of her or his most significant moments, and having you there would mean so much.

Which is a long-winded way of saying someone can be wrong but still take their wrong very seriously and be deeply, profoundly hurt if you refuse to join them in it. Thus a "Sorry, Cannot Attend" RSVP will almost certainly be hurtful, possibly devastating, and may in fact sound a death knell to your relationship with this person. Don't underestimate that when considering how you're going to respond.

So Why Not "Yes"?

Let's look first at the believer's relationship to either nonbelievers or believers involved in ongoing, deliberate, and significant sin.

Having as Good a Relationship as Possible

Regarding nonbelievers, there's nothing in Scripture, or common sense for that matter, indicating we shouldn't have relationships with them. Jesus Himself associated freely and notoriously with sinners or all sorts, showing no compunction about enjoying their company and being among them. (See, for example, Matthew 9:9-12; 11:19;

Mark 2:16-17; Luke 15:1-2; 19:7.) And Paul, writing to the church in Corinth about our differing responses to believers versus nonbelievers, recognized that to avoid relations with non-Christian sexual sinners we'd need to literally leave the world (1 Corinthians 5:10).

He went on, though, to indict being in communion with believers who practice gross, ongoing sexual sin (among other serious sins listed in the passage as well), making it clear that behaviors we tolerate in the world should not be tolerated within the church (1 Corinthians 5:11-12). I have mentioned elsewhere in this book that I do not believe this prohibition commands us to distance ourselves from biological family members; otherwise we'd have to be in violation of other scriptures commanding married couples to stay together and family members to be provided for (1 Corinthians 7:11; 1 Timothy 5:8). In short, I see nothing in the Old or New Testaments advising me not to have as good a relationship as possible with a homosexual family member, believer or nonbeliever.

Being a "Partaker"

The question then is not whether we should have good relations with gay or lesbian family members. We can, should, and probably will. What's at issue here is a particular form of interaction: attendance at a wedding ceremony ostensibly approved of and rejoiced over by those who come to share in it. Attendance means, to my thinking, an offer of approval and blessing.

There's the catch, and it's not minor. Being in relationship is one matter, but participating in, celebrating and, in fact, commending a loved one's sin is another matter altogether. That would constitute violation of Paul's clear instructions to the Ephesians to "have no fellowship with the unfruitful works of darkness, but rather expose them" (Ephesians 5:11) and his advice to Timothy to "neither be partakers of other men's sins" (1 Timothy 5:22 KJV).

Paul's choice of wording here is not accidental. A "partaker," according to Strong's translation of the Greek term involved, is "one who shares, partners, or comes into association with another's activities." And that makes attending a same-sex wedding very problematic indeed.

Broaden the principle to other behaviors and I think you'll see my point. If a brother, sibling, child, or parent I loved had a problem abusing alcohol, surely I would not cut that person off nor look down on him, nor in any way withdraw my love and affection. But if he asked me to go knock back a few brews with him, what else could I do but decline? To do otherwise would mean I would now be not only loving him despite his weakness—his sin, actually—but also participating in it with him. My very presence at the bar, let alone my imbibing alongside him, would say, "I'm with you in this, bro, and I'm okay with it."

Or suppose (to be a bit more ridiculous for a moment) I had a sister who walked on the wild side by occasionally participating in wet T-shirt contests. On the one hand, surely I'd love her, treat her with respect, speak with her, and spend time with her in neutral settings. But could I even for a minute consider accompanying her to one of these events? My presence would clearly message my approval, meaning I would, by being there with her, be saying, "This act of exhibitionism and lust is something I condone and participate in." Unthinkable, of course, and not an option by any reasonable stretch.

The question then boils down to this: Can I attend a homosexual wedding without making a clear statement of support, not only for the people involved, but for the thing itself? Does my attendance constitute friendship and love only, or does it not also testify to approval and outright celebration?

I'd say it does, as attendance at a wedding always does, making it impossible for me to in good conscience show up. For most other events involving a homosexual family member, showing up is certainly an option. If there's a party my family member comes to, my attendance is a statement of my love for him and others, not one of approval for this one part of his life. If we get together under virtually any other circumstances, I see no conflict with Scripture or conscience. But to attend his ceremony would be to say, by my very presence, "I bless and support not only these people, but this event." And that is simply too much.

It would also be too much if a Christian friend of mine asked me to attend his wedding as he united with a nonbeliever, in clear violation of 2 Corinthians 6:14. To be there would be tantamount to saying, "I bless this," when in fact I couldn't. Nor could I show up for the wedding of a Christian friend who dumped his wife for totally unscriptural reasons then latched onto a younger model. Nor, for that matter, would I be okay attending a ceremony for a brother who wildly and irresponsibly says, "God showed me I'm to marry this woman even though I don't know her yet, and she consented so we're getting hitched tomorrow. Be there!"

Because, in all these cases, an event is involved at which attendance equals approval. I see no way around this. If a thing is wrong, no matter how deeply bonded I am to the person involved, although I'm allowed to love and interact with him, I cannot participate in anything expressing approval or support of the wrongdoing itself.

Maybe that's why some Christians feel it's better to attend and maintain the bond than to refuse to come and thereby jeopardize a family relationship. And I'm sympathetic to the sentiments behind that view. If there's any way to avoid a breach in the family without violating our own conscience, then I'm all for it.

But in this case I just don't see any wiggle room. Yes, a Christian may be invited to a heterosexual union of two nonbelievers, a marriage that hardly is, as we would say, "in Christ." But marriage itself is a good thing, ordained by God and beneficial to those involved and culture as a whole (Proverbs 18:22). The same cannot be said for an event claiming to be something that, from a biblical perspective, it simply isn't. Jesus's own reference to marriage was unequivocal:

> Have you not read that He who made them at the begin-
> ning "made them male and female," and said, "For this rea-
> son a man shall leave his father and mother and be joined
> to his wife, and the two shall become one flesh"? (Matthew
> 19:4).

The standard is clear: He who made them from the beginning created the marital bond to be independent, permanent, and heterosexual.
Removing the complementary nature of it makes it something else—a
committed relationship, perhaps, and one in which both parties love
each other deeply. But not, according to biblical standards, a marriage.
Attendance at a ceremony attempting to revise this standard is complic-
ity in the revision itself, qualifying for the warning God issued through
Jeremiah: "Woe to those who call evil good, and good evil; who put
darkness for light, and light for darkness; who put bitter for sweet, and
sweet for bitter!" (Isaiah 5:20).

Deciding on a position, though, is only half the challenge. The other,
which is perhaps greater, is to figure out how to express and hold that
position. When someone you love asks you to attend their wedding, no
doubt it can and likely will be seen as an enormous, even cruel, rejection
if you refuse. So "Sorry, Cannot Attend" will most likely be an insuffi-
cient response. A more detailed and necessary one might, instead, read
something like this:

> *Thank you for thinking of me. The fact you would want to
> include me on a day that is so important to you means so much
> to me, and please know that I recognize what a major event this
> is in your life. You matter hugely to me, and our relationship, it
> goes without saying, matters as well.*
>
> *But if I attended I wouldn't be acting in good conscience
> because, as highly as I think of you and value our relationship,
> I also have inalterable views of marriage, views which don't
> include same-sex unions. I know you don't share my views,*

and in fact they may seem strange or even silly to you. But to me, they're basic, crucial. It would simply be hypocritical and dishonest of me to be there for the ceremony, and I would never ask you to do something you felt would violate your own conscience. You know, I hope, how much you mean to me, and I will always value you and your partner, hoping the best for both of you and always wanting you in my life. I hope and pray, very earnestly, that you'll understand.

May that message, delivered in love and bathed in prayer, bear some good and redemptive fruit when we sadly but necessarily check the box saying, "Sorry, Cannot Attend."

Chapter 9

The Three Most Common Arguments

*Sanctify the Lord God in your hearts, and always
be ready to give a defense to everyone.*

—1 Peter 3:15

So far, we've concentrated more on relationship than dialogue. That's necessary, since having constructive dialogue means first having a healthy relationship. Terms, boundaries, agreements, confessions, and clarifications all need to be made and expressed, paving the way for moving on together with your homosexual family members.

But moving on can also mean discussing differences. So it's likely, if not inevitable, that you'll be discussing many aspects of this issue, such as, What causes homosexuality? How do we determine what's normal or abnormal? Where do convictions end and prejudices begin? These are only a few of the subjects you're likely to encounter in ongoing discussions with a gay loved one. And in the course of them, you may be surprised to learn how many ideas about homosexuality are assumed to be "common knowledge" when in fact they've never been proven. You may also be challenged to re-examine your own beliefs or to throw out stereotypical ideas you might have harbored about gays and lesbians. In other words, you may both learn and teach during these discussions, and that can only be good.

Since no one can predict what topics you and a family member may argue about, no book can adequately prepare you for every conversation.

But in this chapter we'll look at some of the most common pro-gay arguments—ones I think you're most likely to hear and respond to—and offer some comments on and answers to each of them.

Preparing Your Attitude

However, before we look at common pro-gay arguments, let's start with a look at your own heart and the attitude you express during these conversations. Attitude can make or break a person's willingness to listen, so it's always smart to undergo a little self-examination before we speak.

On this subject, the apostle Paul gives us some excellent guidelines:

> A servant of the Lord must not quarrel but be gentle to all,
> able to teach, patient, in humility correcting those who are
> in opposition, if God perhaps will grant them repentance,
> so that they may know the truth (2 Timothy 2:24-25).

If you want your conversations about homosexuality to be productive, don't just prepare your arguments—prepare your *attitude*. You can do so by keeping Paul's concepts of servanthood in mind, so let's consider a few of them.

1. "A Servant of the Lord"

You're not representing only yourself to your family members. If you're openly Christian, you're representing the Lord and, for better or worse, much of what they think about Him will be determined by what they think about you. So keep in mind His characteristics because you're expected to display them if you're going to carry His name.

As a Christian, you represent a loving God who sends rain on the just and the unjust, showing favor to believers and nonbelievers alike (see Matthew 5:45). He compromises neither truth nor compassion (John 1:14), wants all people to be reconciled to Him (1 Timothy 2:4), and has commissioned you to be salt and light (Matthew 5:13-14) while you leave ultimate judgment to Him (Matthew 7:1-2) and consider your own shortcomings before correcting another's (Matthew 7:3-5).

Whew! The servant of the Lord has a pretty tall order to fill. Let's admit it can't be done without prayerful reliance on Him, so we begin with a keen awareness of our dependence.

2. "Must Not Quarrel"

When debating homosexuality with a family member, avoid power struggles. You're not trying to win a case; you're just trying to give a clear presentation of truth. The case is won or lost, after all, in the heart of the person listening to you, and that's a matter between that person and God.

When I hear the way some Christians badger and harp on issues with their homosexual relatives, I'm reminded of what Annie Sullivan told the parents of Helen Keller when she took on the task of teaching their child: "You have so many feelings, they fall over each other like so many feet."

When you feel strongly about a person and are also strongly against what they're doing, you may try too hard, and in the trying, you may be quarreling. I think, for example, of the father who sat in my office telling his adult gay son, "I'll stay on your back day and night until you give this up! What kind of father would I be if I didn't?" I also remember the sisters who demanded their gay brother—a man well into his thirties—give them full access to his computer, phone records, and address book so they could verify whether or not he'd been seeing gay friends. And in less extreme cases, I've seen families refuse to talk to their gay relatives about anything *but* their homosexuality, sending a message that said, in essence, "I can't see you as a person anymore. You're a sexual sinner whom I need to save."

That's not constructive dialogue. It's quarreling, and Paul advises against it because, other than alienating the person you're trying to reach, it accomplishes nothing. *Speak* the truth, by all means, but don't try to *force* it on the hearer. Remember, good stewardship is a cooperative effort between you and God. Your part is to speak; His is to take what you've spoken and open the heart of the person hearing it. Keep the roles straight, and you'll avoid quarreling.

3. "But Be Gentle to All, Able to Teach, Patient"

You can't imagine how strongly gentleness is called for here! To you, homosexuality is an unnatural sin someone you love is committing, and you want to see him restored to a better life. He's someone you value, but the sin he accepts as normal is repulsive to you—you've never been attracted to it or even understood it—so in your mind it's reduced to a set of repugnant sexual acts. When you talk to him about it, you're talking about a *thing* you wish he would give up.

But he sees it very differently. This *thing* you're so repulsed by is deeply ingrained in him, and it's not just a set of sex acts. It's the way he responds both sexually and emotionally, and it's probably been with him for most of his life. He didn't ask for it, he never chose it, and it seems as natural to him as your own sexual responses feel to you. So when you argue against homosexuality as being abnormal or perverted, he feels (wrongly, but strongly) that you're writing him off entirely.

Sugarcoating the truth is not the answer, of course. Believing his feelings are natural to him doesn't make them natural, and their being deeply ingrained doesn't mean God created them. So gentleness does not require us to revise the truth. It only requires a careful, caring attitude when we present it.

Look again at the conversation Jesus had with a Samaritan woman in the fourth chapter of John's Gospel. He recognized she was "living in sin" with a man she wasn't married to, and in recognizing it, He didn't whitewash it. But He saw her first and foremost as a person, not a sexual sinner, and even when addressing her sin, He showed gentleness and respect.

So when you speak, follow Him. It's not enough to know what's right or wrong. Servanthood requires showing the gentleness He showed. Remember John's admonition and take it carefully to heart:

> He who says he abides in Him ought himself also to walk just as He walked (1 John 2:6).

God help us, then, to walk—not just talk—the Christian life.

Common Pro-Gay Arguments

Let's look at three general, common pro-gay arguments you're likely to hear from a homosexual family member. I'll present each by first stating the argument, then by giving some background on the cultural and emotional influences contributing to it. Next I'll offer a few points to keep in mind, and finally I'll give a sample response—an example of common points and counterpoints I've heard over the years—to help give you an idea of what sorts of dialogues you can expect to have. So the model we'll follow will be

- argument
- background
- points to consider
- sample responses

Of course, every conversation is unique. I don't suggest you mouth these arguments word for word, nor should you expect your conversation to follow these sample dialogues to the letter. But I hope they will get you better acquainted with points that will be raised in your discussions. That in turn should better equip you to respond to them.

"I Was Born This Way"

Argument. I was born this way. I've been gay as long as I can remember, and I can't change. I've tried. I've even been to counseling, been prayed for, read books, and done all anyone could do to change, but nothing worked. So I can only assume this is the way I was born, and this is the way God intended me to be.

Background. As I mentioned in chapter 2, the idea of homosexuality's being an inborn condition is relatively new. When Alfred Kinsey surveyed homosexual patients in the 1940s, asking them how they thought they became homosexual, only 9 percent claimed they were born that way. Thirty years later, a 1970 survey of 979 homosexuals conducted in San Francisco found that nearly the same low percentage felt their orientation was something they were born with.

After another 30 years, how things have changed—not through *enlightenment* (which is the reason ideas normally evolve with time) as much as by *repetition*. As the gay-rights movement has become more aggressive, it's brought with it concepts that have been repeated often enough and broadly enough through a media largely sympathetic to the pro-gay view—to the point that people have come to accept them as being true without examining them. And the inborn theory is one of the most common of these oft-repeated, never proven, yet widely believed ideas.

And politically, it's a useful label. After all, many people assume "inborn" and "natural" are one and the same. So if the public can be convinced homosexuality is inborn, that will go a long way toward convincing them it is also natural and, therefore, morally acceptable. In fact, the inborn theory has successfully placed homosexuality in the same category as race in many people's minds. And since America is keenly aware of the evil of race discrimination, we're sensitive to the plight of any mistreated minority.

Thus, if homosexuality is inborn and if homosexuals have been subject to discrimination based on something as genetic and immutable as skin color, then opposition to homosexuality becomes akin to white supremacy. That's the strategy, and so far it's worked.

Yet in fairness, you should also consider what it's like to have feelings or tendencies from early in life and then try to change them, only to find them (in many cases) stubbornly, consistently *there*. When something is deeply ingrained and resistant to change and began early in life, it's easy to assume it's something you were born with. That's a simpler and, in many ways, easier belief to live with than the idea that someone would choose to be gay. So when your gay family member claims to have been born homosexual, he's probably not just falling back on a political convenience. It is most likely a deeply held belief.

Points to consider.

1. As of now, it has not been conclusively proven that homosexuality is inborn. In fact, there are doctors, scientists, and mental-health specialists—some of whom are openly gay—who reject the idea that homosexuality is genetic, seeing it instead as something created by a variety of influences, both genetic and environmental.

2. Some studies have shown that sexual orientation is not necessarily fixed, so the assumption that homosexuality cannot be changed is certainly open to question.

3. What is right or wrong—or normal versus abnormal—isn't determined by what can or cannot be changed. Nor can it be determined by what is or is not inborn. Any number of abnormal conditions or immoral behaviors might be traced to genetic links. Alcoholism, violence, and depression may all be at least partially created by inborn factors, and there's solid evidence that genes play a role in their development. Yet we'd never redefine "normal" or "healthy" to include these behaviors or conditions. So the fact that a tendency is deeply ingrained, difficult to change—even inborn—does not legitimize the tendency itself.

Sample response. You may be right. No one knows for sure what causes homosexuality, so genes may have something to do with it. I believe you when you say you've felt this way for a long time, and maybe that means this is something you were born with.

But when you compare your cause to the civil-rights movement, with all due respect to whatever injustices homosexual people have suffered— and I know there've been many—they can't be compared to the struggles African-Americans have endured.

Gays and lesbians weren't kidnapped from their homelands and shipped here in chains. They weren't bought and sold like cattle, nor were they put to forced labor as slaves. They've never, in this country, been considered someone else's property, nor has it ever been legal in America to beat, torture, or kill them. There have never been "gay" and "straight" drinking fountains, theaters, and parks, nor have gays ever been denied the right to vote, own property, or attend the same schools as heterosexuals. In other words, there's simply no comparison between the two groups.

But just because I don't equate it with race, that doesn't mean I think homosexuality is a choice. I know you didn't ask to be attracted to the same sex. And I believe you when you say you've tried to change these feelings, but they're still with you. From all I know about human sexuality, it seems our sexual responses, whether they're good or bad, tend to be pretty deeply ingrained. And sometimes, no matter how hard we try, we can't change them.

Then again, many people have walked away from homosexual behavior and either stayed celibate or moved on to heterosexual marriages. Most of them report they're still tempted, some more than others. They may still have homosexual attractions and fantasies. Some relapse, the way some people "fall off the wagon." Some have even given up and returned to homosexuality as a way of life, claiming the desires and thoughts are too strong to resist.

But isn't it true of most people that we have desires or thoughts we wish we didn't have? That doesn't mean we have to yield to them. So when you say you can't change, I guess I'm not sure what your definition of "change" is. If by change you mean a complete transformation of sexual feelings, then maybe that's too strict a definition. You can definitely change your behavior, and in most cases you'll find that if you do, the desire for that behavior will at least decrease.

This may all sound like nonsense to you. Why, you might think, should you even try to change? And maybe that's where the real difference in our thinking lies.

You seem to think what comes naturally to you is therefore natural. You feel you're not harming anyone by being gay, so no one should object. And if I didn't believe we have a Creator to answer to, I'd agree with you.

But I believe we're created beings, and I believe the Bible—a document that's been a best seller for centuries and still heavily influences much of Western thought—spells out the Creator's plan for the human experience.

I also see in the Bible that God had a specific plan in mind when He created sex, a plan for a union between a man and a woman that's complementary. I think the way our bodies are made attests to that plan, and I think it should be carefully considered before anyone abandons it.

And ultimately, that's why I'm less concerned with what a person may or may not be born with. The human race is imperfect and, according to the Bible, fallen. That means we're born with imperfect natures, so we're not physically, emotionally, or spiritually what we were meant to be.

What matters in the long run isn't what we were born with or without. Rather, it's what God expects of you and of me. That—not what comes naturally to us—should determine our definition of "normal."

"You're Homophobic"

Argument. You've inherited a prejudice against gays and lesbians that's so prevalent, you can't even see it! Like most people, you've been taught that homosexuality is unnatural, so you object to it because you're part of a culture that's homophobic. What you call "moral objections" are really fears, ignorance, and misconceptions all wrapped up together. It's *homophobia*, not homosexuality, that's the real problem here.

Background. *Homophobia* is a word that's been cleverly used to paint anyone who objects to homosexuality with the broad brush of bigotry. It's a relatively new word, first coined by psychologist George Weinberg in 1972, and originally intended to mean "dread of being in close quarters with homosexuals." Thirty years later, its meaning has broadened considerably. It now is used to apply to any person, expression, or belief that does not place homosexuality on par with heterosexuality. And because it's such a negative term, like "racist" or "sexist," it intimidates many people and keeps them from speaking against homosexuality. After all, who wants to be seen as a bigot?

Points to consider.

1. The term *homophobia* doesn't hold up to scrutiny. *Homo* means "same"; *phobia* means "dread or irrational fear. The word *homophobia* means, then, "dread or fear of the same," whatever that means!

2. Even if we concede the point linguistically and consider the term a description of fear or dread of homosexuals or homosexuality, it still doesn't hold up in most cases. After all, if a person is speaking face-to-face with a homosexual, relating to that person, and interacting with him, then that person could hardly be said to have a dread or fear of homosexuals. If he did, such a conversation, much less such a relationship, would be impossible.

3. To be sure, there is such a thing as prejudice against homosexuals. Many people have an irrational belief that they are superior to gays and lesbians and that homosexual people are inherently inferior, second-class beings. But the belief that homosexual behavior is immoral is neither a phobia nor a prejudice. It's a belief based on a simple, well-established worldview, and it neither discriminates against nor demeans homosexual people.

Sample response. Disagreeing with me is one thing, but labeling me because of my views is another. It's unfair and a little below the belt. So let's both try to avoid resorting to names and labels, okay?

I have no phobic response to you or to homosexuality. Think about it, please—have you ever seen an arachnophobe? A person with that condition has such a dread of spiders that he can't be near one. That's what phobias do to people. But I'm sitting right here with you, aren't I? If I had a phobic response to you, this conversation wouldn't even be possible.

And I have to plead not guilty to the charge of prejudice too. Yes, I think homosexuality is a sin. And if I thought that made you a worse sinner than I, then I would be guilty of prejudice. But I don't think that. You seem to feel that if I believe something is a sin, I also believe myself to be sinless. Far from it! In fact, if we were to compare personal sins, I could probably come up with a list longer than yours.

But believing homosexuality is wrong is a belief, not a prejudice. If you think I've treated you as though you're inferior, I want to know it, because believe me, that's not the way I feel. When I talk to you, I'm one imperfect human speaking with another—nothing more or less. So please don't write me off as having a condition just because we disagree. Beliefs, prejudices, and phobias are three completely different things that should never be lumped together.

"Gay Marriage Is Valid"

Argument. My partner and I love each other and are as committed to each other as you and your spouse are. It's wrong to see us or treat us any differently than you would any other couple. To say you can't recognize our relationship the way you would if it were a heterosexual one is discriminatory and wrong! We expect you to see us and treat us as you would any married couple.

Background. Until recently, the idea of two men or two women marrying each other seemed remote at best. But now, same-sex marriage is well on its way to becoming a reality in America as, state by state, new rights are being granted to homosexual couples—rights that for centuries have been recognized as uniquely appropriate for men and women in the establishment of strong families—a critical building block of a healthy society.

But the issue isn't as cut-and-dried as you may think. Although many gays and lesbians hope for the day their relationships will become state-sanctioned, many others oppose the very idea of assimilating into the heterosexual mainstream. Some feel gay marriage would be a sellout or a way of becoming more like "straights" instead of retaining the rebel status of those outside the majority. And some, like gay apologist Andrew Sullivan, have freely admitted that, if homosexual relationships become recognized as marriages, the way marriage itself is seen and experienced will be radically altered.

Added to the mix is the sincere belief many gays and lesbians have about their partnerships. In many cases, they sincerely love each other and are committed to their relationships. They invest, build, and grow old together, and they cannot understand why it's so hard for those of us who oppose homosexuality to see their relationships as being no different from ours.

But because the notion of same-sex marriage is so clearly at odds with Scripture's definition of marriage and normal sexual relating, from a biblical perspective it's impossible to recognize a gay partnership as you would recognize a marriage. You may tolerate a gay loved one's relationship; you may choose to socialize with a gay couple; you may do your best to retain good relations with them. But you cannot with integrity call that relationship a marriage.

And therein lies the tension growing by leaps and bounds in families around the world. As more and more same-sex couples demand that the term "marriage" be applied to their coupling, the more divisions the issue will create, because more and more families feel compelled to either revise their view of marriage or suffer loss of harmony with their gay loved ones. Your home, unfortunately, may become one of these battlegrounds. Because, whatever boundaries you choose to draw when it comes to family gatherings, you won't be able to say yes to the demand for a redefinition of marriage.

Points to consider.

1. *You can recognize that people love each other, and you can respect their right to form a partnership even if you disagree with the nature of their partnership.* To say a relationship is wrong is not to denigrate the people involved in that relationship.

   For example, I have often compared gay relationships to the relationship actor Spencer Tracy had with leading lady Katherine Hepburn. Tracy was a married man when he met Hepburn, yet they fell in love and, by all accounts, were deeply committed to each other for decades although they never married. It's entirely possible to recognize two glaring and somewhat conflicting facts about their relationship: It was adulterous, therefore wrong; and love was involved. They cared deeply for each other, and there were no doubt many good things to be said about their relationship. To say it was morally wrong does not equate to a refusal to recognize those good things. But to recognize those good things cannot change the fact it was morally wrong. The two are not mutually exclusive.

(I know—at this point you might argue over what does or does not constitute real love, and I would agree. But I find it more useful to clarify an even more important point: Love does not, in and of itself, justify a relationship or a behavior.)

So it is with gay couples. Your objection to homosexuality is not a dismissal of whatever love or commitment may exist between your gay loved one and his or her partner. Despite your objections to homosexuality, you recognize that they have every right, as freewill agents, to enter into this relationship, and you're aware there may be deep levels of commitment and devotion involved in it.

But you're also declaring it's a relationship God cannot sanction, so neither can you. You can respect those involved, but you cannot in fairness be asked to revise ancient standards to accommodate people you otherwise respect. That's where the line has to be drawn.

2. *As with arguments comparing homosexuality to race, comparing our current objections to same-sex marriage with objections raised in the past against interracial marriage is also unwarranted and inaccurate.*

It's true that at one time in American history, marriage was forbidden between Caucasians and African–Americans. However, this was not a restriction that had strong historical precedent. Interracial marriage was, in fact, nothing new and had been present and practiced in many cultures for centuries. So while America was wrong in prohibiting marriage between people of different races, it was not prohibiting something that had never been tried.

Same-sex marriage is quite different. It's not only something we *currently* object to—it's something that's *never*, until recently, been recognized in *any* culture as a legitimate marriage. That's the difference between same-sex marriage and interracial marriage. Marriage between races was not unprecedented; it did not constitute a great national experiment. Gay marriage certainly does, and the results so far (unlike those of interracial marriage) are not hopeful.

In the Netherlands, for example, after two years of government-sanctioned same-sex marriage, the municipal health service of Amsterdam reports that marriage relationships among young Dutch homosexual men last from one to one and a half years, and that "extra union" contracts (which allow for additional sexual partners besides one's married spouse) are common. Eight of such "extra union" contracts per year is the average.[1] Such an arrangement cannot be, by any reasonable standard, in the best tradition of marriage. Nor can it possibly be in the best interest of the children involved.

3. *Statistics and cultural concerns aside, redefining marriage is especially unacceptable to the Christian*, as marriage is spelled out in both Testaments as a type of God's relationship with His people (see Isaiah 54:5; Jeremiah 31:32; Ezekiel 16:21-32; Hosea 2:19; Ephesians 5:25; Revelation 21:2).

To redefine something that so clearly represents the unchangeable nature of God's relation to His people is unthinkable to any serious believer.

If the man represents Christ and the woman represents the church, then a male-to-male partnering would be, in essence, a symbolic partnering of God with Himself apart from His people. Likewise, a lesbian relationship would become a symbolic partnering of God's people without Him. Either option is incomplete, unnatural, and abhorrent.

Sample response. This may be the toughest issue for us to come to terms on. It may divide us permanently, although I hope it doesn't. But here's how I see it:

I take what you say at face value when you say you're in a committed relationship and that you love each other very much. Our definition of love may be different—maybe you see it as a combination of affection, bonding, and commitment, while I see it as all of those—so long as they exist in a relationship sanctioned by God. But no matter—I know people have the ability to love in a variety of relations, and I realize two people of the same sex can love each other very deeply.

So from your perspective, my refusal to call your relationship a marriage, and my refusal to say I recognize you and your partner the way I would a heterosexual marriage, seems bigoted and ridiculous. You see it as a complete denial of everything good you two have and as a way of saying you're second-class citizens, not deserving the same respect others have.

But you're wrong on all points. I don't deny there's good in your relationship, nor do I think you're second-class. Yes, I disagree with you on sexual ethics, but it's unfair to say disagreement and bigotry are the same! They're not. I'm fully aware you have a relationship that means very much to you. So I can call it a relationship; I can say there's love in it; I can respect your right to live as you please. But I cannot and will not call it a marriage.

Calling a homosexual partnership a marriage is an entirely new concept, and it's one even gays and lesbians aren't in full agreement on. Can you honestly tell me I'm bigoted for having reservations about something that many homosexuals themselves have reservations about? Be fair! No culture has ever defined a same-sex relationship as a marriage. Even cultures that openly condoned homosexuality didn't consider it to be part of the marriage institution. So at the very least, you have to admit my view is a common one. It certainly doesn't put me in the category of a wild-eyed bigot.

So if you're demanding I call your relationship a marriage, I have to refuse. I love you, respect you, and certainly don't want to lose you. But if our relationship forces me to choose between you and the truth, what do you honestly expect me to do? I'll never go out of my way to demean you or your partner, and I'll always treat you both with consideration. But I won't say one thing when I believe another. I would never ask you to do that. So please, as an adult and as someone I care about, don't ask it of me.

The above three examples are typical of the discussions you will have (and may already have had) with your family member. Other topics may come up as well. Your gay loved one may argue any of the following:

- "The American Psychiatric Association considers homosexuality to be normal."

- "Up to 10 percent of the population has always been homosexual."

- "People who hold your antigay views actually inspire others to attack gays and lesbians."

- "I'm a gay believer, and I feel it's fine with God."

- "Jesus said nothing about homosexuality."

- "The church has been wrong about women and African–Americans in the past; now it's wrong about gays."

- "The writers of the Bible didn't understand what we now understand about homosexuality."

- "The Bible really doesn't condemn homosexuality; it's just been mistranslated."

All these arguments, along with others, are presented and answered in detail in my book *The Gay Gospel?: How Pro-Gay Advocates Misread the Bible* (Harvest House, 2006). So if these topics are coming up in your family, pick up a copy. I think you'll find it helpful.

Do's and Don'ts for Discussions

Let me close this chapter by offering a few do's and don'ts when discussing homosexual issues with your family members.

1. *DON'T attack the character of homosexual people when you argue against homosexuality. Keep the two separate.*

    Some Christians are prone to regard homosexuals luridly—as being, by and large, potential child molesters and left-wing anarchists. That's not only untrue, it misses the point: You're arguing about homosexuality itself, not the nature and character of homosexual people.

    Attacking someone's character rather than sticking to the issue is always a sign of a weak argument. The issue is not whether or not homosexuals can be good, worthwhile people. The issue is whether or not homosexuality is, in and of itself, normal and moral. Keep the focus clear.

2. *DO admit when and where the church has been wrong.*

    After all, the church is far from perfect. So when I'm discussing this issue with an openly gay man or woman, I'll be the first to admit that, in many cases, Christians have poorly represented Christ by showing more judgment than concern toward their gay friends and family members.

    I find this strengthens rather than weakens my argument. Because when I argue that homosexuality is wrong, I do so based on the teachings of Scripture, not the track record of the church. So admitting the flaws in Christians is by no means a concession. Instead, it puts the focus where it belongs—on the issue, not the personalities of the people involved.

3. *DON'T resort to clichés or pat answers when you discuss such an important issue.*

Remarks like "God made Adam and Eve, not Adam and Steve" sound trite and make the person who says them look like someone who hasn't thoughtfully examined the issues. Clichés are for ads and political campaigns. In serious discussions, avoid them.

4. *DO avoid the phrase "the gay lifestyle." There's no such thing.*

Gays and lesbians lead many different types of lifestyles, ranging from celibate, to committed, to the raunchy and wild. Your family member will be rightfully insulted if you assume that, because a person is gay, such a person must automatically live a certain way. This too is a sure way to lose credibility. Remember, your objection is to homosexuality, not to a particular lifestyle, and no one lifestyle represents the way all homosexual people live. Many heterosexuals live wilder lifestyles than homosexuals.

5. *DON'T be discouraged if your conversations aren't bearing the fruit you hoped they would.*

Your job as a servant is to speak truth plainly, lovingly, intelligently. That—not your loved one's response—is what you will answer to God for.

God grant that, when you take a loving stand for truth, you'll see the fruit of your labors in this life and the reward for them in the next.

Chapter 10

Reasoning Together: Ten Additional Talking Points

"Religion is as necessary to reason as reason is to religion. The one cannot exist without the other. A reasoning being would lose his reason, in attempting to account for the great phenomena of nature, had he not a Supreme Being to refer to.

—George Washington

When someone you love is outside God's will, the answer to the problem lies within that someone, not in your arguments, pleadings, or tears. If something doesn't happen in the heart and mind of that person, softening the one and enlightening the other, then there's no reason to assume she or he will ever be back within God's will. If a sheep will not be shepherded, all the efforts of the other sheep can't make it happen.

That's the bad news, and it's pretty bleak. The good news, of course, is that the Shepherd who loves your loved one so deeply is still active, still engaging, still calling that person to Him. And although you cannot make that person respond to the Shepherd's call, you can, by His grace, be part of the formula that eventually turns a life around and brings a prodigal home. It does happen—which is a hope, not a guarantee. How, when, and where will it happen? We've no way of knowing. What we can know is that God often uses simple human conversation—human reasoning, if you like—to engage a person's mind and ultimately soften the person's heart. And if you can be a part of that process, so much the better.

So it may be that your conversations with your son, daughter, or sibling will be used to further God's purposes. As a steward of truth, you thereby want to be prepared for such conversations, and that's why this chapter is here.

The bulk of this book has been about negotiating the relationship, establishing mutual understanding and boundaries as needed, and dealing with your own emotions in the process. But as I pointed out at the beginning of the previous chapter, having done so, you and your loved one are still likely to have conversations about this. If you live together this is especially true, considering that gay-related news stories are likely to come over the television and Internet, political issues relative to the subject are likely to be featured in the paper and other media, and family conversations are at some point likely to hit on the topic as well. Avoiding the subject of homosexuality is hard these days; it's a hot-button issue that's simply not going away.

At times, of course, it's prudent to drop it. When discussions about homosexuality keep getting heated and family members are consistently alienated as a result, I say it's time to call a moratorium. Likewise, if you find that whenever you bring the topic up your loved one shuts down, then I'd say you're banging your head against the wall. You don't have to talk about it. There've got to be other things you can focus on as people who love and enjoy each other, and there can be real wisdom in deciding to avoid something you know will stir up strife while offering little or no benefit. In fact, I've encouraged a number of families to drop it altogether and opt instead to concentrate on enjoying each other as much as possible, rather than needlessly rehashing the topic over and over.

Then again, there really can be a place for ongoing discussion. After all, both you and your loved one know the issue is there, a notable elephant in the middle of the living room, comfortably settled and unmoving. You want your homosexual family member to see the elephant as an unwanted intrusion; he wants you to see it as a benign pet. If you both can talk out your feelings and concerns, and the talks are productive rather than simply argumentative, terrific.

When the conversation begins, there are a number of statements you're likely to hear. In this chapter, I've listed ten common questions or statements raised by homosexual family members. After each statement I've listed a few talking points to help guide you in your response, hoping to better equip you to first think each point through, then articulate a calm, reasoned response in your own words. I sincerely hope these points will be useful to you.

Ten Talking Points
for Ongoing Discussion

Statement One

"If you don't approve of homosexuality, then you don't accept me."

1. That's an impossible standard to live up to because no one approves of everything in another person's life. In the best of relationships there are areas of disagreement.

2. That's an immature standard to set up because it demands complete agreement or complete rejection—no middle ground.

3. God loves all of us, but surely you don't think He approves of everything about us!

4. I do not assume that, because you disapprove of my beliefs about sexuality, you thereby reject me. If I don't hold the issue up as a litmus test of acceptance, why should you?

5. Judge my acceptance of you by the way I treat you, not by what I believe about one aspect of your life. And I'll do the same for you.

Statement Two

"No one can 'pray away the gay,' so what choice do I have?"

1. I would never ask you to simply "pray away the gay." If you feel homosexuality is right and normal, then obviously you won't try praying it away.

2. I don't believe you can simply "pray away" unwanted feelings. I have plenty of desires and tendencies I wish I didn't have, but I find strength to deal with them even though they remain in spite of my wish they would leave.

3. "Pray away the gay" is essentially a media term that has little or nothing to do with people who sincerely repent of homosexual behavior. Most of them freely admit that the temptations may remain, and so they pray more for the strength to deal with those temptations, rather than simply trying to pray them away.

4. You don't have a choice about what turns you on sexually, but you do have a choice to either resist or express your sexual desires. We all have that capacity, and most of us deal, to some degree, with unwanted attractions toward people we cannot legitimately have a sexual relationship with. That doesn't make us helpless; we still decide to say *yes* to some feelings and *no* to others.

5. The apostle Paul himself had an issue he sincerely prayed to be delivered from, and God's answer to him was to refuse to remove the problem and, instead, allow His grace to sufficiently equip Paul to live with it and thereby glorify God in his area of

weakness (2 Corinthians 12:7-10). If that was true of him, why can't it be true of anyone else?

Statement Three

"If God wanted me straight, then He would either have made me that way or changed me when I asked Him to."

1. While it's true that we're all created by God, we're not all He created us to be. Ever since the Fall, mankind has been beset with feelings and experiences we were never meant to have (Genesis 3:16-19).

2. Plenty of deeply ingrained tendencies are symptoms of the flesh, not the spiritual nature, so we shouldn't assume God created them (Galatians 5:19-21).

3. Honest believers will admit that, despite all kinds of earnest prayer, they continue to have feelings they wish they didn't have. I've got plenty of those myself! But we never assume that, just because we have deeply ingrained feelings that have stayed with us even when we asked God to take them, we should therefore now indulge them.

Statement Four

"Plenty of churches are now accepting gays. Why can't you?"

1. What makes you think we don't? Have you seen a sign on our church door saying, "Gays: Stay Out"? We welcome anyone who wants to attend our church.

2. If someone wants to join our church as a member as opposed to just attending, then we do require that person to be living a life submitted to biblical standards. And we believe biblical

standards do not allow for any form of sexual relationships outside heterosexual, monogamous marriage.

3. We do teach the traditional view on human sexuality, which includes a disapproval of homosexual behavior. That hardly qualifies us as "not accepting gays." I think a more honest way of making your point would be to say we don't *agree* with gays, rather than we don't *accept* them.

4. We do not condone homosexuality because of clear biblical standards explaining what God intended the sexual union to be (Matthew 19:4-5) and clear prohibitions against homosexuality itself (Leviticus 18:22; 20:13; Romans 1:26-27; 1 Corinthians 6:9-10; 1 Timothy 1:9-10). There are also clear prohibitions in scripture against adultery, fornication, incest, and prostitution, and we adhere to those as well.

5. We take our direction from Scripture, not church trends. The fact other churches embrace something is not, therefore, a compelling reason for us to do so.

Statement Five:

"My love for my partner is just as strong as yours is for your spouse."

1. That may well be. I've never implied that you and your partner don't love each other.

2. I don't believe that love alone validates a relationship. My wife could fall deeply in love with another man and in fact love him more passionately than she's ever loved me. That would not justify the relationship; it would still be adulterous.

3. It isn't fair to assume that just because I do not approve of your relationship, I therefore cannot see how important that relationship is to you.

Statement Six

"The fight for gay rights is the new civil-rights movement, and you're on the wrong side of history."

1. It seems unfair to compare gay rights to civil rights. Racists in the past considered African–Americans to be inherently inferior to whites, whereas Christians who believe homosexuality is a sin do not believe homosexuals are essentially inferior to heterosexuals.

2. The comparison of African–Americans to homosexuals doesn't hold up well. Homosexuals were never kidnapped and transported in chains to this country, nor were they ever bought and sold here. We've never had gay and straight drinking fountains, nor have homosexuals been denied the right to vote, use public facilities, or stay in hotels or eat at restaurants.

3. Racists denigrate the entire personhood of minorities. Conservative Christians affirm the personhood of all people while recognizing they have sinful tendencies and believing some behaviors to be right and others to be wrong. That's a far cry from the all-or-nothing mentality of racists.

4. Being "on the right side of history" is not my goal. Holding the position I believe to be true, and holding it in the most loving and clear way possible, is my goal.

Statement Seven

"Your viewpoint causes depression and suicide among gay people."

1. The way this viewpoint has been expressed by some Christians is in fact hurtful, and I'm sorry for that. But it isn't fair to assume that because *some* Christians have presented the traditional view in a hurtful way, *all* Christians who present the traditional view are therefore being hurtful.

2. Expressing a belief that a thing is wrong does not cause depression in people. Expressing it or enforcing it in the wrong way can—and there's a big difference.

3. Suicide among gay people is a tragedy we'd all like to prevent. We won't prevent it by muzzling people who hold differing viewpoints. Instead, we should express our viewpoints with respect and consideration.

Statement Eight

"Your viewpoint inspires violence against gays."

1. There's no solid evidence that teaching the traditional viewpoint on homosexuality encourages anyone to commit an act of violence against a homosexual.

2. The people who assault homosexuals are generally not Bible-believing, churchgoing Christians. They express a hatred of homosexuals because they believe gays are different, and churches do not teach either that hatred or that belief.

3. If teaching or preaching against a certain sin caused people to commit violence against those practicing that sin, then why don't churchgoers go out after their Sunday services and assault liars after they hear a sermon against lying? Why don't they go out and assault prostitutes after hearing a sermon against lust and fornication? This argument simply doesn't stand up, because preaching against a behavior does not cause people to mistreat those involved in that behavior.

Statement Nine

"We're both believers, but this is just a minor issue we disagree on."

1. I don't dispute the fact that you're a believer. I'm sure we agree on other essential issues, I don't question your sincerity, and

believe me, if a matter really was nonessential, I wouldn't let it come between us. But if after careful study I conclude that homosexual behavior is a sin, then I have to treat it with the seriousness with which Scripture calls us to treat all sexual sin.

2. Sexual sin is never considered a minor issue in Scripture. Paul described it as a serious offense against a person's own body (1 Corinthians 6:16). The first recorded case of church discipline in the Bible occurred over a sexual matter (1 Corinthians 5). And immorality is one of a select few behaviors that do, according to Paul, draw lines between believers (1 Corinthians 5:9-11). Also, most books in the New Testament specifically address the subject in clear, unambiguous terms. That being the case, we could hardly call sexual sins a minor issue.

3. By its nature, this issue cannot just be about homosexuality. It also encompasses the way we define the family, the way we conceptualize marriage, and how we interpret and apply the Bible. Those are hardly minor issues.

Statement Ten

"Jesus said nothing about homosexuality."

1. We do not define something as right or wrong simply because it was or was not addressed by Jesus. He did not specifically address bestiality or spousal abuse in the Gospels; surely we wouldn't therefore conclude that these behaviors could be legitimate!

2. We don't take our guidance from the Gospel accounts alone; otherwise there'd be no need for the rest of the New Testament or any of the Old Testament. All of Scripture, then, is inspired

of God, and is authoritative and instructive (2 Timothy 3:16-17).

3. Jesus did refer specifically to God's intentions for marriage and the sexual union in Matthew 19:4-5, clarifying that marriage was intended to be monogamous, permanent, and heterosexual in nature. Anything falling short of that standard is, by virtue of its falling short, a sin.

More Resources for Discussions About Homosexuality

The Gay Gospel?: How Pro-Gay Advocates Misread the Bible by Joe Dallas (Harvest House Publishers, 2006)

The Complete Christian Guide to Understanding Homosexuality by Nancy Heche and Joe Dallas (Harvest House Publishers, 2010)

"Speaking of Homosexuality" by Joe Dallas, *Christian Research Journal*, May 24, 2013, www.equip.org/articles/speaking-of-homosexuality/.

"The Bully Pulpit—When Gay Teens Commit Suicide, Are Christians to Blame?" by Joe Dallas, *Christian Research Journal*, May 24, 2011, www.equip.org/articles/the -bully-pulpit/.

Chapter 11

A Mile in Their Shoes

He jests at scars that never felt a wound.

—Romeo and Juliet

Two weeks before starting to work on this chapter, I got a useful but very unwanted lesson in empathy. While stopped for the red light at one of my town's major cross streets, I heard a *crash/boom!* directly behind me. A split second later, my car was hit and hurled into the intersection, making me the third vehicle in a three-car collision. Evidently, the driver behind me had tried to make a left turn without noticing the car approaching behind *him*. That car slammed into him, he slammed into me and, thankfully, I slammed into no one. But I'd been hit—and hard.

My first reaction was shock, very much like denial. I could hardly believe what had happened, and in the immediate aftermath, I went into autopilot: pulling my car over, checking myself for injuries, then hurrying across the street to exchange information with the other two drivers.

But after calling the police and making the necessary reports, anger kicked in as I realized that, because of someone else's actions, *my* plans were put on hold, pain was inflicted on *me*, and I would now suffer because of a problem I had neither created nor asked for. As I write this, my back and neck are stiff, I'm getting chiropractic adjustments each week, and my damaged vehicle needs repair. In short, my life has been disrupted by someone else's sin.

No doubt some bargaining is yet to come, as my insurance company negotiates settlements with the company covering the man who hit me. And depending on how serious and chronic my back and neck problems become, I may even deal with a bit of depression. Acceptance, I can already tell, is a ways off.

But in the midst of my mini grief process, some feeling for the man who hit me is creeping in. Yesterday, for some reason, I remembered how sorry and frightened he looked and how many times he apologized and admitted, both to me and the reporting officer, that he was entirely responsible. And only now am I also remembering his shaking his head, telling me he had never had a worse day, then recounting with tears how his wife of seven years had just come to his office to announce she was leaving him for another man.

Small wonder he was so inattentive at the wheel! Yet at the time I was so focused on the problems he'd created for me, I scarcely considered what he was going through. I'm not the only one who's suffering, though up to this point, I've acted as though I were.

Can you relate to any of this? You too were going about your business, then—*crash/boom!*—homosexuality hit home. When it did, it was hard to see beyond your own disappointment and pain and think about what your loved one has been through, what he's feeling, what he was experiencing long before the crash. You may care about him deeply, but having never walked a mile in his shoes, your care may be without understanding. And he knows it. He knows you're clueless as to what it's like to be homosexual, and he takes that into account while listening to your antigay arguments. He may know you believe his homosexuality is a sin, but he also knows how little *you* know about the sin you're condemning.

Trying to Understand

In Shakespeare's *Romeo and Juliet*, young Romeo, before meeting Juliet, is deeply in love with a woman named Rosalind, who doesn't return his love. The play opens with Romeo pining away for her, and his friend Mercutio teasing him for being so lovesick. Realizing Mercutio knows nothing about being in love, Romeo says of him, "He jests at scars that never felt a wound." His friend, in other words, is observing and commenting on a condition he has no understanding of. And that lack of understanding makes Mercutio, in Romeo's mind, unfit to judge.

Fair enough. But when it comes to homosexuality, what sort of understanding can you be expected to have? There are plenty of other sins you relate to, but most likely this is something you've never experienced, so is it fair to expect you to relate to it? And even if you did, would that change your beliefs on the matter?

No, nor should it. But when you object to another person's behavior, your objections will carry more weight if you've at least *tried* to understand what led to that behavior in the first place. It won't change your mind as to what's right or wrong, but it will increase your compassion, and your credibility as well.

I noticed this when I first read *A Tale of Two Cities* by Charles Dickens, a story I enjoy rereading every few years. By drawing an up-close portrait of women and men involved in the French Revolution, Dickens lets us walk a mile in their shoes long before the bloodbath begins. He writes about their wretched daily lives in a way that draws us into their hard world, and we learn to care about them. We watch them scrape out a bare living in horrible conditions, we feel their suffering and want, and after witnessing so many of the injustices they face at the hands of cruel aristocrats, we share their rage at the system that keeps its boots firmly on their chests. By the time the Revolution begins and the tables are turned, we are (at first) cheering them on. Only later, when they become as cruel to their former oppressors as the oppressors had been to them, do we begin to criticize them. But when we do, we remember what gave birth to the wrong we condemn, even as we condemn it.

So should you, and you can by walking a mile in the shoes of your gay loved one. So in this chapter I'd like you to use your imagination and try walking through some of the life experiences that usually go along with being gay. It won't give you a *perfect* understanding, of course, but it will give you a *better* one. And a better understanding of another's experience strengthens your ability to show grace to that person even as you stand for the truth. (Remember, the challenge to display both grace and truth is one we set for ourselves at the beginning of this book.)

What's It Like to Be *Different*?

So first, imagine you're a child who's *different*. Not just unique in hair color or temperament, but in ways that are unacceptable in the eyes of others. There's nothing inherently wrong with you, but from early in life you notice that you don't (as is often the case with prehomosexual children) share the same interests many of your classmates have. If you're a little boy, your peers like team sports and Westerns, for example, while you may be drawn to books and Broadway musicals. They're aggressive and social; you're quieter and more sensitive. Or maybe you're creative in areas they're not, and you enjoy things they, for the most part, don't. So big deal—you're different. Is that a problem?

You soon find it is, as you learn that, for some reason, being different is not okay. You start hearing the same questions from schoolmates, teachers, and even parents: "Why aren't you more like *that* and less like *this*?" Of course you've no idea why, so a shrug is the best answer you come up with. But you're starting to feel that being like *this* instead of *that* makes you guilty of some deliberate crime against nature, which does nothing to enhance your self-confidence or personal comfort. You've got a few strikes against you, but you're not sure why.

I remember experiencing all this, as do many of the women and men I've known over the years who've dealt with homosexuality. Mind you, I loved playing football as a boy, and I was a Dodgers fan who attended games regularly. But I also loved music, books, and plays. Moreover,

I was very sensitive, easily hurt, shy, and vulnerable. I wasn't aware of being homosexual, just *different*. And when other kids picked up on the difference, the blood they smelled in the water whipped the little sharks into frenzies.

That's when the teasing begins: "That's *sissy*! You act like a *girl*! That's *weird*!" Or if you're a little girl, it's "That's what *boys* do!" or "Why do you dress like that?" With this teasing comes an awful realization: Whatever it is that made you different is not going away, others are aware of it, and you're marked. You're guilty of what is clinically known as gender nonconformity. But on the playground, which has little in common with the safety of a clinic, it's better known as the crime of *differentness*. And there's a good chance your gay loved one was punished for this unchosen differentness without fully understanding why. Or without *your* knowing about it.

Stop and consider this: The person you love has probably felt different—set apart from others—from very early in life. Most adult homosexuals will attest to this. And the rejection from being different *hurt*, especially since the difference wasn't a fault or a sin, yet he or she was made to feel it was. So where does a child go, and to whom does a child turn, when he or she is in pain over something barely able to be defined, much less understood?

"Different" Becomes "Cursed"

Now keep walking. Let's go from early childhood to adolescence and imagine now that the difference has become a curse.

You've been aware of your "differentness" for some years now. Maybe you've even gotten used to it or at least found ways to deal with it. But now another element is being added to the mix of your life.

You probably won't refer to it as puberty; you may not even know it has a name. But you know your body is changing, and along with your peers, you're experiencing strong erotic attractions. Like them, you begin having romantic fantasies. You develop crushes on schoolmates, you become fascinated with sex, certain movie stars or musicians become the objects of your daydreams—and you hear, in the conversations you either have with other kids or overhear the other kids having, that you and they are experiencing the same thing.

Well, *almost*. Because, of course, everything they're saying—their descriptions of the people who turn them on, their boasts about "how far they went" on a date, the crushes they report, and the notes they compare about classmates and celebrities—all have to do with the opposite sex. You feel just as sexually attracted as they feel, but for people of your own sex. It's a feeling you certainly did not choose; it's one you've discovered. And having discovered it, you learn to cover it up, carefully and quickly.

That's because, just about the time you realize you're homosexual, you also realize it's one of the worst and most dangerous things to be. Or so it seems. Remember, adolescence is a time when the opinion of your peers is crucial. Much of your self-confidence and sense of worth is derived by how "in" or "out" you feel with them. Their judgment carries weight. And on this subject their judgment is harsh and outspoken. You hear them throw out words like *faggot*, *dyke*, and *fairy* when they want to insult someone in the worst way. And even if you don't initially know what those words mean, you know that whatever they mean, it must be something pretty bad.

"So-and-so is a fag," you hear; "stay away from him." Or, "She's a dyke; can't you tell? She acts just like a guy." And suddenly, it seems everyone is talking about gays. You hear jokes and one-liners about them; classmates talk about beating them up; rumors fly as to who may be one of them. And you find it hard not to conclude that people talk in the worst possible terms about *them* when they want to feel better about themselves at the expense of someone else.

Then you finally learn what *faggot* means, and you do the math. You compare your own private sexual feelings to the definition of a faggot or dyke, and you're confronted with the horror of being one of *them*. "Different" has now become "cursed."

Stop again and try to remember a time you had a dark, scary secret. Something dreadful you did that you hoped no one would discover. Or some private habit you were truly ashamed of, which you knew would make you disgusting in the eyes of friends and associates. Suppose it was something people often talked about in front of you, not knowing you yourself did "it." Try imagining your shame as you listened to them express their contempt for people like you as they joked about "them" and basically congratulated themselves for not being like "that." And suppose that, as they described people like you as "perverts," "freaks," and "queers," you stood there nodding and smiling, praying nothing you said or did would give you away. Imagine your feelings in the dark later that night as you considered how little the world seemed to think of you and your kind. Can you feel the loneliness, even the desperation, of the outcast?

I did, and recalling it chills me to this day. As a boy, I heard my father laughingly brag about beating up "queers" when he was a young man and how proud he was to hurt them. I responded with a sick, weak little grin, acting as though I understood and approved, but already knowing that something in me was very similar to whatever Dad so hated in those "queers." And of course, that meant something about me was terribly wrong and completely unacceptable.

In junior high, by which time I was very aware of my own sexual confusion, it seemed I'd entered into an echo chamber of fag jokes. My coaches, classmates, friends, and teammates all seemed locked into an antihomosexual contest, vying (or so it seemed to my increasingly paranoid thinking) to see who could make the cruelest remarks about gays and who could concoct the worst punishment for "them." Terrified someone would suspect one of *them* was present, I'd join in, adding my own voice to the chorus of hate for people like me. My early sexual conquests of girls helped my status, of course, and by bragging about them, I kept anyone from suspecting the unthinkable. But I knew, and I agonized. My friends thought I was one of them, but I knew I was one of *them*.

And I so wanted not to be one of *them*. I prayed and waited to outgrow those feelings. I tried analyzing myself to discover what dark part of my psyche I could adjust to make myself normal, but finding so many dark parts, I finally gave up, overwhelmed. Ask your gay loved one if he or she has ever felt this, and ask what it was like. Let your loved one tell you about pretending, hiding, hating, and disapproving of himself while at the same time dying for approval. Walk in his shoes—walk slowly through this part, especially—and you'll learn something invaluable about the life and pain your loved one has endured.

Spiritual Conflict

Don't stop there, though. Let's walk now through the spiritual conflicts so many homosexuals experience. "What about his relationship with God?" family members often ask me. "He was raised in church; he knows better! How could he throw all that away?" "She *knows* what the Bible says about homosexuality. How can she embrace such a perversion?"

The simplest answer is, your loved one misunderstood, then gave up.

The first misunderstanding may have been about God's feelings toward him or her as a person wrestling with private homosexual longings. Try imagining yourself as a Christian teenager, keenly aware of your attraction to the same sex and equally aware of your church's position on those attractions and the people who have them. You're a committed believer (don't even ask me to count the number of parents who've described their gay son's or daughter's early zeal in the church!), and you truly want to serve God, so you can't understand why these feelings even exist.

At first you think you simply need to repent of them, so you try. But to *repent* means to *turn,* and how do you turn away from sexual responses? Of course you learn not to give in to them, but you know they're still *there.* And that, you fear, is a sign of God's disapproval. After all, you hear time and again how evil homosexuality is, so how could a true Christian even have these feelings? You misunderstand, assuming that God is displeased with you and that you're a second-rate believer who's essentially flawed.

So you pray harder, remembering the many Scriptures you've heard since childhood about answered prayers. Again you misunderstand, and this time your misunderstanding has to do with the nature of prayer and human struggle. Surely, you think, if God hates this sin so much, He'll relieve you of any temptation toward it. And as you're waiting for that relief, you hear Christians—your own pastor, perhaps, or well-known radio or television preachers—talk about homosexuals. You hear about their agenda, their aggression, their threat to the family, their future eternity in hell. You sense the contempt and the anger so many in your church feel toward the gay-rights movement and, by extension, toward gays themselves. And all the while your prayers to change from gay to straight aren't being answered.

Now you begin misunderstanding people as well as God. You'd love to talk to someone, but who? Considering the anger so many Christians seem to feel toward *them,* you're not at all sure you're ready to admit you're one of *them*, even though you're repentant and have nothing in common with gay-rights activists and advocates. You assume—wrongly, in many cases; rightly, in too many others—that Christians would look down on you for having homosexual desires even if you're committed to not acting on them. So now you not only believe God sees you as flawed, but you extend that assumption to others' beliefs as well.

So you're scared and alone, a terrible combination. You're afraid to tell your family because you don't want to hurt and worry them. You won't even consider telling your friends, as you're certain they'd ostracize you. But maybe you take a risk and disclose your struggle to someone—a youth pastor or some other adult you feel you can trust—and maybe you get some good advice. Or maybe not. You may be advised (as many of my clients have been) to solve the problem by playing sports or wearing makeup (depending on your gender, of course), or by reading a book, resisting the temptation to masturbate, fasting, participating in a deliverance session, or by keeping quiet and sweeping the whole darned thing under the rug because no one knows what to do with it.

Meanwhile, you're getting older, ready to graduate high school and begin college or a career, and the long hoped for "I'll outgrow it" hasn't happened. Again, you misunderstand. You feel betrayed by the God who didn't answer your prayers for deliverance and by the church that seems to condemn homosexuality while offering little or no help to the condemned. And so, misunderstanding much about God and the community of believers, you might give up on the faith altogether.

Wrong move, of course. Unanswered prayer (or at least, prayers that weren't answered in the way we hoped they'd be), inadequate counsel, or the imperfections of other believers are no excuses for quitting. But before criticizing, walk a bit in the confusion and frustration your loved one experienced for years beforehand, and remember how hard he tried, prayed, and struggled before finally shifting from "I Surrender All" to "I Quit."

A Place to Belong?

Move on, now, as you reach early adulthood and start hearing about an entire community of people like you. There are any number of ways you gain access to this community—Internet chat rooms, gay bars, campus clubs, gay churches—and what you find there is revolutionary. You no longer feel so different; you find commonality, a new experience for many young homosexuals who've never felt anyone understood them. You find unity with others who've shared your struggles and fears and a strong sense of purpose and identity within the gay community. You belong (finally!), and you rejoice in the relief and strength belonging almost always brings.

Now, having found a population of people who seem comfortable being gay and who live, in most ways, responsible and relatively normal lives, you begin questioning the beliefs you've held for so long about homosexuality. *Is it really wrong?* you ask yourself; *and if so, why?*

Those two questions alone are enough to open a floodgate of other questions you may have been afraid to ask anyone, even yourself. But among supportive people who believe your long-held secret feelings are perfectly normal, you begin discussing the many issues homosexuality raises.

"I've felt this way for so long; could I have been born gay? And if I was, doesn't that mean God made me that way? And if God made me that way, wasn't it crazy for me to try to change what God Himself created? And if God Himself created it, aren't all the others—my family and the church, for example—aren't *they* the ones who were wrong all the time, instead of me?"

And, of course, at almost any university, or gay support group, or modern social setting, you're quite likely to hear the very answers you're craving:

"*You* were never wrong. *They* were!"

The relief your loved one experiences upon hearing that—relief from years of self-doubt and fearful, lonely struggles—is incomprehensible. Believe me, for him, this coming-out process may be the most profound, exhilarating experience of his life, as he decides the difference is no longer a curse; it's a gift! And thus a huge weight is lifted.

Call it deception, self-justification, immorality, or plain old rebellion, and you'll be correct. But don't call it any of those things without at least trying to walk in his newfound, albeit false, sense of freedom. What looks to you like the death of integrity feels to him like a literal rebirth.

"I Have Something to Tell You…"

Now walk with him as he considers coming out to you, and walk with respect. After all, he's thinking about you, remembering all you are to him and the history and love you share. He's had a major change of heart and mind, and his lifestyle choices reflect that change. So maybe he's coming out to you because he's involved romantically and doesn't want to hide it; maybe he's taken up gay activism and is considering going public, so he wants to give you fair warning. Or maybe he's just reached a point where he wants to be honest with the people he's closest to, including you.

For whatever reason, then, he's decided to tell you he's gay, and he's wondering *how*—how to say it, how you'll respond, how the two of you will go on from here. He's probably fearful since he knows this is information you won't want to hear. He talks it over with his friends: How did *they* come out to their families? How did *their* loved ones handle it?—and he practices his "Folks, I'm gay" speech, trying to find the right words. And believe me—he is troubled about your possible reaction.

Don't overlook the obvious: He's troubled because he loves you! He has no desire to hurt you, and *hurt,* he knows, is a moderate word for what you'll feel when he makes his announcement. Yet he also feels the need for honesty and wants to avoid lying to you, directly or indirectly. So a large part of what drives him is the desire for his relationship with you to be honest and genuinely close, even if that requires facing the hard truth.

He knows your position on homosexuality. He knows you'll worry about him, pray for him, argue with him, and hope to change him. He expects all that, but fervently hopes you'll accept him, as well, and that you'll not let this new information negate all the good that's existed between the two of you.

However, coming out to you is also a final step in his journey toward self-acceptance as a gay man (or her journey as a lesbian woman). He sees this not only as an exercise in honesty but also as a way of being true to himself and his cause. He's scared, but for him this is a ritual of independence, a final statement of identity and purpose. So recognize, as you walk with him right up to that *crash/boom!* moment when he finally tells you, just how much blood, sweat, and tears went into *his* preparation for the event that propelled you to pick up this book—when he said, "I have something to tell you..."

Walk in his shoes. Listen to his words and consider all that has led up to them. Read and reread the chapters in this book that are relevant to you, pray for wisdom and direction, and then, having walked a mile in your loved one's shoes, ask him or her to now walk in yours. To that end, let me offer a sample letter for you to use in any way that's helpful as you look for words to express all that's in your heart for the person you love... the person whose homosexuality has hit home, and whose home is now wanting to express both its love and its concerns.

A Letter to My Loved One

We both know there's a time for silence and a time for speech. I've tried to keep silent while letting you speak. I've listened to your beliefs, your decision, your desires, and your reasoning. I've walked a mile in your shoes, and in doing so, I've learned. I ask now that you return the favor and walk with me as I try to make sense of all that's in my heart.

By coming out to me, you've asked for honesty in our relationship, even if it means painful honesty. So be it. In the spirit of such honesty, it makes no sense for me to pretend your coming out of the closet was anything but devastating to me. And yet I know, and will never forget, how hard it must have been for you to say those two little yet huge words: "I'm gay."

You knew I didn't want to hear it, yet you had the courage to tell me. And yes, I do recognize the courage involved, and the integrity as well. Just because we disagree on homosexuality itself doesn't mean we can't find common ground in other areas. We can both appreciate honesty; we both know it's better to be open about your life than to pretend; we both value what's commonly called *being real*. For that reason, I thank you for telling me. Yes, it crushed me. Still, I recognize you were respecting me, and certainly trusting me, when you told me. If I haven't thanked you for this before, let me thank you now. Thank you for daring to believe enough in me—and in us—to let me in on your life.

And I'll not return your honesty with anything less on my part. Your announcement was a death sentence in many ways. So many of my dreams for you died upon hearing those two words. The children I imagined you having, the marriage I thought you'd live and die in, the way of life I thought you were committed to—all flashed through my mind, then expired horribly when I considered what the phrase "I'm gay" really meant. You haven't died of course, nor has our relationship or the love we'll always share. But those dreams have died, and what can I do but grieve them? They've been a precious part of my expectation for you for so many years. So please hear my pain, even if you think it's groundless, because it's now so much a part of me that you can't recognize me without recognizing it as well.

If I reacted harshly when you first told me, I not only ask your forgiveness, but I ask a bit of understanding as well. No one lets go of their expectations easily, so when you told me you are gay, my expectations, like my dreams, died. So I lashed out. I was angry at you for deciding that what God forbids is now something you accept and that what you once believed was wrong is now, in your eyes, right and normal. I suppose, though, I was also lashing out at life for dealing me a blow I never expected. Perhaps, God forgive me, I was even lashing out at Him for allowing something I never thought He'd allow.

At any rate, my words may have been harsh and mean-spirited. Yes, I'm convinced you're utterly wrong about homosexuality, but you don't deserve to be treated with anything less than respect and consideration. So whenever or wherever I've failed to show you that, I apologize. And please understand this: The depth of my anger only shows how deep my feelings are for you. That's no excuse; just an observation. After all, if you didn't mean so much to me, your announcement wouldn't have meant that much either.

But I've thought your announcement over. I've considered what you've told me about your life so far—how you tried to change but couldn't; how you feel you've finally found yourself; and how wrong you think I am for holding on to beliefs that seem to be held by fewer and fewer people. And having considered all this, I'd like to respond.

I believe you when you say you feel you were born gay. We can argue all we like about scientific studies and what they do or don't prove, but no one can argue with experience. So if you say you've felt this way from early in life, I understand. But even if that were so—and I'm not saying it is—does it really matter? When did you decide that just because something is inborn, it must therefore be normal? Aren't we all born with imperfections of some sort? And for that matter, how is it you decide what is or is not normal or moral? At one time, I believe you took your cues on morality from the Bible. But now it seems you look more to subjective experience when making your ethical choices. You seem to say, "If something seems natural to me, it is therefore natural. If I can't change my desires, I must therefore legitimize them. And I am the final authority on what is or is not right for me, so long as I do no verifiable damage to another." And let me tell you plainly, that scares me.

It scares me because, although you say you're becoming more like your true self, I see you instead becoming a god to yourself. You establish right or wrong based on your subjective experience; you say that if you can't change, you must accept rather than deny your true feelings; and you say (or seem to say) that self-acceptance overrides everything else. On the other hand, I remember a time you believed obedience meant more than self-acceptance, and that what was right or wrong was determined by a higher authority than our feelings and experience.

When and how did your thinking change?

I will, sadly, agree with you when you say many Christians don't handle this subject well. I'm so sorry for whatever cruel or thoughtless things anyone has ever said to you. I'm sorry that when you struggled with this privately, you didn't feel you could talk to me. Believe me, had I known you needed me, I would have been there for you. But how could I have guessed what you were going through? In that sense, I suppose we both suffered.

But is it fair to say all Christians are unreasonable, just because of the wrongness of some? In all fairness, those of us who believe homosexuality is wrong hold that belief not out of some prejudice or hate but out of a serious reflection on what the Bible says about God's intentions for humanity. So please—just as you've asked me not to write you off because of the outrageous things some gays have done—don't you write me off just because of the wrong things other Christians have said or done to gays. Most of us, after all, know the difference between acceptance and approval. We can accept each other freely even if we don't approve of everything the other does.

So even as I accept you, joyfully and fully as someone I love and hold dear, I can't accept much of your reasoning. You say God let you down when He refused to take away your homosexual desires, so you've decided either He isn't worth serving or perhaps He approves of the very feelings you were trying to get Him to remove.

Well, if I lived my life by that standard, I can tell you many things I'd be doing. I'd still be overeating because, since God never took away my desire for junk food, He must either be unreasonable—or maybe He wants me fat! I'd be blowing my stack whenever I wanted: Since God never removed my temper, that must mean He approves of tantrums!

I know I sound sarcastic, but will you grant me this at least? Please reconsider your expectations of Christianity. You seem to have forgotten it is not a system put together to make us feel good about ourselves or to help us find happiness and self-acceptance in this life. It's about believing on Him and, having believed, following Him. Did you really think following someone who died sacrificially would require anything less than sacrifice from you? My greatest fear for you, at this point, isn't generated by your homosexuality. It's generated instead by your belief that life is about fulfillment rather than obedience. And I truly believe that is a self-contradicting irony that offers neither fulfillment nor obedience.

We have much to negotiate. We'll have to decide how to relate, how to visit, who may or may not be included and under what terms, when (if ever) to argue about this, and above all, how to love each other and protect our love even as we differ. That's no small challenge we're facing, but I'm up for it. And in so saying, I'm committing myself to preserving our relationship. I promise you my respect and my affection, always. My beliefs and my love are both unchangeable, so take them both if you want to take me.

My heart is both broken and full; my door is and will remain open to you; and hope is steadfast. God, who loves you infinitely more than I or any human could, will continue to work in your life. I've committed you to Him, and I am persuaded He will keep and redeem what is committed to Him. In this, and in the love and bonds I hope we'll always share, I find my peace.

❧　❧　❧

God grant that peace to you, the reader, even now. God grant you all the wisdom, patience, and faith you'll need when homosexuality hits home. And let me personally thank you for the honor of walking with you during this difficult time. As someone on whom neither God nor family gave up, let me offer my prayers and love, and my hopes to hear from you as you and your family walk this difficult road. May we all walk it as He did: steadfast, purposeful, and always full of grace and truth.

What to Do Now

Life has changed for you—forever—with the announcement of your loved one's struggle with homosexuality. Hopefully for you, the change will be a little bit easier because you've read *When Homosexuality Hits Home*. But this book isn't meant to be the final word for you on your new journey. There are many other fine resources and ministries that can help you continue to walk this unfamiliar path. Below are just a few. I'd encourage you to make use of the ones that seem most appropriate and, if possible, find support from others who understand what you're going through. Many people with homosexual loved ones have found support from the Restored Hope Network (restoredhopenetwork.org) and other similar ministries.

Suggested Reading and Resources

For men struggling with same-sex attraction:

> *Desires in Conflict* by Joe Dallas (Harvest House, 2003)

For women struggling with lesbianism:

> *Restoring Sexual Identity: Hope for Women Who Struggle with Same-Sex Attraction* by Anne Paulk (Harvest House, 2003)

For parents and family members with homosexual loved ones:

> *Someone I Love Is Gay* by Bob Davies and Anita Worthen (Inter-Varsity Press, 1996)

101 Frequently Asked Questions About Homosexuality by Mike Haley (Harvest House, 2004)

Splashes of Joy in the Cesspools of Life by Barbara Johnson (Word, 1992)

Living Stones Ministries
www.livingstonesministry.org
(626) 963-6683

Parents and Friends of Ex-Gays (PFOX)
www.pfox.org
(703) 360-2225

To refute the pro-gay biblical interpretation:

The Gay Gospel? by Joe Dallas (Harvest House, 2006)

To discuss and debate issues related to homosexuality:

The Complete Christian Guide to Understanding Homosexuality by Joe Dallas and Nancy Heche (Harvest House, 2010)

Homosexuality and the Politics of Truth by Jeffrey Satinover (Baker Book House, 1996)

Help for sexual addiction:

The Pure Restoration four-day seminar for men, conducted and taught monthly by Joe Dallas. Contact Pure Restoration:

1-888-580-PURE (7873)
www.purerestoration.com

To contact an organization in your area offering ministry to homosexuals:

Restored Hope Network
www.restoredhopenetwork.org

National Association for Research and Treatment of
Homosexuality
(818) 7789-4440
www.narth.org

Notes

Chapter 2: How Can This Be?

1. Warren Throckmorton, "Homosexuality and Genes: Déjà vu All Over Again?" website of NARTH (National Association for Research and Therapy of Homosexuality), www.narth.org/docs/dejavu.html.

2. W.D. Fairbairn, "A Revised Psychopathology of the Psychosis and Psychoneurosis," *Essential Papers on Object Relations*, Peter Buckley, ed. (New York: New York University Press 1986), p. 83.

Chapter 4: When Your Teen Says "I'm Gay"

1. Dallas, Joe, "The Bully Pulpit: When Gay Teens Commit Suicide, Are Preachers to Blame?" *Christian Research Journal*, volume 34, number 03 (2011). http://www.equip.org/articles/bully-pulpit-gay-teens-commit-suicide-preachers-blame/#christian-books-3.

Chapter 5: When Homosexuality Hits Your Marriage

1. Willa Medinger as told to Bob Davies, "Facing my Deepest Fears," 1984, 1998, website of Exodus Global Alliance, http://www.exodusglobalalliance.org/facing mydeepestfearsp12.php.

2. Mary Ann Hastings, *A Woman and a Homosexual Man: The Good Thunder in My Life: A Testimony and a Workbook for Women Who Love Homosexual Men* (no city: 1st Book Library, 2000), no page number available.

3. Kathy Gilmore, "God Saved my Marriage," in Sheri Stone and Therese Marszalek, *Miracles Still Happen* (Tulsa, OK: Harrison House, 2003), pp. 142-146.

Chapter 8: Same-Sex Weddings: "I'll Be There" or "Sorry, Cannot Attend"?

1. For a fuller treatment of the pro and con sides of this issue see Michael Ross and Joe Dallas, "Should Christians Attend Same Sex Weddings?" *Christian Research*

Journal, October 15, 2012, www.equip.org/christian-research-journal/should -christians-attend-same-sex-weddings/.

Chapter 9: The Three Most Common Arguments

1. Maria Xiridou (of the Cluster of Infectious Diseases, Municipal Health Service, Amsterdam, the Netherlands) et al., "The contribution of steady and causal partnerships to the incidence of HIV infection among homosexual men in Amsterdam," *AIDS Journal* 17:7 (May 2, 2003), pp. 1029-1038, retrieved June 24, 2014, http://archive.today/mgOT#selection-1015.0-1015.84.

More Insightful Resources on Homosexuality from Harvest House Publishers

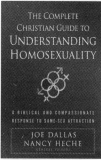

The Complete Christian Guide to Understanding Homosexuality

A Biblical and Compassionate Response to Same-Sex Attraction

Joe Dallas and Nancy Heche

What do you say to someone who's gay?

Many Christians—pastors, parents, counselors, teachers, co-workers, perhaps just good friends—are grasping for an appropriate response to this hot-button issue. But it *is* possible to extend God's love toward those with same-sex attractions while holding firmly to biblical truth. And a first step toward offering hope and support is learning more about homosexuality.

In this well-researched and highly readable guide, you'll discover answers to the difficult questions people ask:

- Is the tendency for homosexuality genetic?
- What's the proper response when relatives or friends announce they're gay?
- How do I explain homosexuality to my young child?
- What should churches do to offer hope to homosexuals?
- How does homosexuality affect society?

These questions and many more are answered in this authoritative and comprehensive guide to homosexuality from a Christian perspective, written by authors who are not only are experts but also have the necessary personal experience to bring the compassionate touch of Christ to their research.

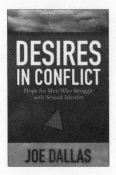

Desires in Conflict

Hope for Men Who Struggle with Sexual Identity — *Joe Dallas*

The conflicts are real.

- The desire to love God vs. the desire to be loved in a way God prohibits
- The desire for a normal sex life vs. the desire to satisfy feelings that seem normal—but aren't
- The desire to be transparent vs. the desire to avoid the pain of misunderstanding

So are the solutions. You won't find any quick fixes in this book. What you will find is effective help for restoring sexual wholeness and moving ahead in life with God.

Desires in Conflict is a groundbreaking resource not only for men who struggle with their sexual identity, but for anyone who cares about a family member or friend struggling with homosexuality.

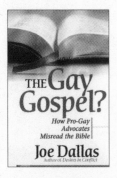

The Gay Gospel?

How Pro-Gay Advocates Misread the Bible
Joe Dallas

For six years Joe Dallas was both actively gay and a church-attending Christian. But deep within, he was bothered by one huge question: "Am I basing my decision to embrace the 'gay and Christian' identity on the belief that this is God's *will* for my life…or on the hope that this is what God might *allow*?"

That question caused him to take another look: not just at what *he* wanted out of life—but at what *God* wanted for him.

From this unique personal perspective on the pro-gay Christian movement, Joe provides

- a thorough background in the development and nature of the "gay gospel"
- a concise but detailed understanding of pro-gay theology's beliefs
- a clear biblical response to each belief
- a practical, compassionate plan to bring truth to people who believe "gay" and "Christian" are compatible
- and the essential balance between conviction and compassion

Restoring Sexual Identity

Hope for Women Who Struggle with Same-Sex Attraction
Anne Paulk

"Very early in my life, I felt the tug of sexual attraction toward some of my own sex. I remember being both confused and excited...and also very unsure...Then, in college, after many years of having been attracted to other women, I embraced a lesbian identity and lifestyle. A short time later, after an encounter with God, I began my journey out of homosexuality..." —*Anne Paulk*

Here are answers to the difficult and often wrenching questions asked both by women desiring change and by friends and relatives of women struggling with same-sex attraction:

- Is lesbianism a genetic predisposition or is it developed during childhood?
- Does becoming a Christian immediately eliminate all desire for members of the same sex?

- What support is available for women who struggle with lesbianism?

- Can a woman be a lesbian and a Christian at the same time?

- How does childhood sexual abuse relate to the development of lesbianism?

For every woman sexually attracted to other women…here's another choice.

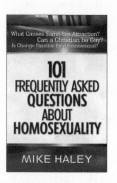

101 Frequently Asked Questions About Homosexuality
Mike Haley

- We just found out our child is gay. Is it our fault? Did we do something wrong?

- Can a homosexual really change?

- Our pastor says that all homosexuals are going to hell. Is he right?

- I'm a single mother with two sons. How can I reinforce their identity as men?

- I have a hunch someone I know is struggling with homosexuality. How do I approach him about this without pushing him away?

For many, homosexuality isn't just a societal issue…it's very personal. A son or daughter reveals a longstanding struggle with same-sex attraction, a husband leaves his wife for another man, a co-worker shows up at the office picnic with her female lover.

Here are answers to the questions about homosexuality so often raised by these situations and others—fielded by *Focus on the Family's* Mike Haley, a former homosexual and an expert on the subject.